Behind Their Smiles

An Adoptive Mother's Journey From Trauma To Triumph

Pamela White-Taylor

Printed in the United States of America

First Printing, 2018

ISBN-13: 978-1727890532

ISBN-10: 1727890531

Special Thanks

I would like thank the many friends and family who traveled this journey by my side. Many of you were present in my life long before our adoption took place and watched this amazing adventure that changed every part of me. Thank you for your unconditional love and support.

My Husband Mac:
To my best friend who has held my hand every moment through this crazy journey we call life. I never imagined that God would lead us down so many different, but truly rewarding paths. Thank you for your willingness to step out in faith with me and risk everything to follow God's will. I can't thank you enough for your quiet and calming presence in the midst of all the storms and for your willingness to love me unconditionally over the years. I am so honored to call you my husband and the father of my children. I am proud of the man you are and look forward to watching you continue to change lives. I love you more than I could ever express.

My Sons - Trent and Mike

You boys have changed every part of me. The gift of becoming your mother has been the greatest blessing I have ever received. I thank God each and every day that I can call you my sons. Thank you for allowing me to walk this healing journey by your sides and for loving me so deeply. I am beyond proud of both of you for not letting your trauma define you. Instead, you are allowing God to use your past as a means to help others. You are my heroes! I am truly honored to be your mother and cannot wait to watch you boys change the world around you! I love you both more than you could possibly imagine.

Mom and Dad

You have shown me what the love of a family truly means as you have supported me throughout my entire life. You have selflessly put my needs ahead of your own time and time again. I have always rested in the comfort of knowing that you will always be there to hold my hand, offer encouraging words, or give me the warming hug I need to continue pushing forward. I cannot remember a time when you have not dropped everything when I needed you. Your unwavering love and support through this adoption journey are what got me through the most challenging time in my life. I love you both more than words can express and am so proud to be your daughter.

Isaac and Ashley Gomez
We have had many friends come and go over the years, but you have remained by our sides despite the craziness. Throughout our adoption journey, you were a strong support and dropped everything when needed to watch the boys, provide emotional support, and offer help. Thank you for being a constant positive force in the lives of Trent and Mike and for serving as godparents. You are family! We love you both.

Diane Bunn

Thank you for serving as a social worker and putting your heart and soul into ensuring that Trent and Mike received the permanency they deserved. Your job was not an easy one, but you did it with honor! We will be forever grateful to you.

Tina Morris

Thank you for having the courage and dedication to see Trent and Mike through very difficult times. Your willingness to put your heart and soul into your job and work on behalf of children in need is a true inspiration. Our family is forever grateful for you!

Doreen Arnott

I am so thankful for your friendship and for your dedication to our family and to Mercy for America's Children. Your compassion and devotion are unmatched. I am so blessed to have you in my life. Thank you for serving as editor and helping me complete this book.

Author's Notes

In order to protect anonymity, names in this book were changed. This book was written from the perspective of an adoptive parent with the intent to help others as they learn from the experiences of a mother who traveled a journey with her children from trauma to triumph. Since this book was written to inspire hope and not to harm, all identifying information has been changed to protect the privacy of those involved in the story.

Note To Families

This book was written to help those who have been through trauma as well as those who are supporting or raising children who have experienced trauma. While the majority of the book is age appropriate for all, the content is very emotional and may be difficult for some to read. Parents are highly encouraged to read the book prior to providing it to children. They may also want to consider reading it with their children. Various forms of abuse are discussed in a very general format but may be uncomfortable for younger readers.

I also wanted to note that as a professional who works in the area of foster care and adoption, I strongly believe that reunifying children with their birth family members is always the best scenario if it is safe and healthy. Reunification should always be the initial goal. In our situation, reunification efforts were ceased in the courts after many years of supports and interventions were implemented and failed.

Lastly, our adoption story tells of a very emotional and difficult journey. The reward was worth every tear that was shed, and I would complete each step of it again without hesitation. In no way do I want this story to discourage others from entering the process of fostering or adopting. Instead, my desire is that this story will provide a sense of hope and deliver an understanding of how facing trials in life with trust in God's plan can change the path one walks and empower an inner strength not known to exist. God has given me proof that this is true; because I have traveled down this difficult road, Mercy for America's Children was created.

About the Author

Pam is an adoptive mother of two boys who have changed her life in unimaginable ways. After a very complicated adoption process, Pam resigned from a 17-year career as a special education teacher to pursue her passion of forming a non-profit organization that promotes and supports the adoption of children in the foster care system. In 2012, Pam and her husband, Mac, founded Mercy for America's Children. Pam serves as the Executive Director for this thriving organization. She has an extensive background in Child Development and Behavior Analysis and trained at Texas Christian University to become a practitioner in Trust Based Relational Intervention. Her background has proven very valuable when supporting families who are fostering or adopting through the foster care system. Pam has successfully led this organization which is now very well known across the state of North Carolina. Pam has been recognized for her accomplishments and was named "Woman of the Year" by the National Association of Professional Women in 2014. In addition, she has been recognized by Who's Who Among American Business Women and was named a "Woman of Influence " by the International Women's Leadership Association. Most recently she received the Albert Neilson lifetime achievement award. Pam has a true heart for children and families and has dedicated her life to promoting positive change in her community. Most importantly, Pam has a heart for God and strives to do His will.

In addition, Pam and her 17 year old son, Trent, work together in a speaking ministry called "Watch Me Rise". They travel across the country to tell their story of healing to both small and large groups. Their story has become a powerful tool that provides hope to those who are fostering or adopting. Pam and Trent plan to publish additional books and training materials to assist others through the healing process.

Table of Contents

Prologue

When I look into a carefully crafted bird nest, I wonder about how difficult it must be for baby birds to take that flying leap of faith off the edge and trust that they are ready to flap their tiny wings and soar on their own. For so long, they have been safely snuggled in the warmth and comfort of the home that was lovingly created by their mother whom they trusted to provide them with food and safety each day. Eventually, the babies are forced to muster every ounce of bravery and confidence they can dredge up in order to take the courageous leap off the edge of the nest and soar into the real world where they must then care for themselves.

While the baby bird must experience tremendous fear, I often wonder about the feelings of the mother bird who has spent every ounce of her being creating a safe and loving environment for her babies, keeping them safe and warm, and has working tirelessly each day to gather worms to make sure their little fuzzy bellies are full. How must she feel as she watches her babies fly away after she has given them every part of herself? She must experience a true flood of mixed emotions as the wonder of the babies' first flight takes place.

As I watch my children grow, I am not unlike the mother bird. I have spent the past 8 years giving of myself each day to make sure that my babies are provided a safe and nurturing environment and that they are loved unconditionally each day. Ultimately, I want to prepare them to soar. However, watching them grow so quickly is difficult, knowing that someday soon they will take that frightening leap into the real world. Will they possibly be ready? How will they function without me? The fact is that they have only had parental guidance for the past 8 years. Is that enough time to instill morals and values, teach compassion and help them learn how to function in this harsh environment that our world has become?

Although I no longer think of my sons as being adopted (they are simply my sons), the reality is that they spent 6 and 8 years of their precious lives without me. They were not provided with the comfort of a protective and nurturing nest for the first part of their existence.

Instead, they were consumed by fear, doubt, and a long-lasting inability to trust adults to provide them with basic necessities such as food, clean clothing, and safety. They learned at a very early age that they could not rely on adults to meet their basic primal needs. Even worse, they learned that adults were not safe and could not be trusted. While time has healed some of these wounds, some scars that remain serve as reminders of past pain. We have learned to view this pain as a part of our healing journey as a family. It has helped us grow as individuals and as a family unit.

Our family was not created in a traditional manner. Adopting older children through the foster care system came with many ups and downs. Many of those challenges helped us become strong. I would not exchange this journey for anything: it changed every part of me. It was a path full of trials and we journeyed some dark roads, but have now entered the light on the other side of healing.

I am so proud of my family and feel a love for them that I am truly unable to describe. Trent, Mike, and Mac. This is dedicated to you, Team Taylor. I thank

God each and every day that I have been given the gift of being wife and mother to such amazing men.

The Moment

The moment had arrived. I glanced around the courtroom and shuttered as I recalled all the information that had been exposed in court over the past 4 days. We had spent countless hours hearing testimony from therapists, social workers, and Guardian's Ad Litem. We had also witnessed painful testimonies delivered by various birth family members. The chaos of the week sank in as I recalled different memories from the previous days: being escorted out of the courtroom through secret corridors by armed police, meeting and talking on the phone in secret, threatening glares from across the courtroom. We had endured each and every moment in an effort to fight on behalf of the boys who had been ours in our heart from the moment we met them. This was the long awaited moment in time that determined whether or not I would be granted the gift of becoming mother to two boys who were nothing short of miraculous. Although I did not give birth to them, I knew in the depths of my soul, from the moment we connected, that they would become ours.

I glanced down at the dog tag that was adorning my neck and ran my fingers across the engraved words. It had become a symbol of bravery, patience, and hope. The tag was inscribed with the verse, "For I know the plans I have for you, plans to prosper you and not to harm you, plans to give you hope and a future." I stealthily tucked the token into my dress as we prepared to hear the final verdict from the judge who had been entrusted with deciding the fate of two boys who had experienced a living hell during the most crucial years of life. After a total of 4 days in court, everything came down to that defining moment. The room was painfully silent other than sounds resonating from the air conditioning unit that was attempting to cool the overheated courtroom. As I gripped Mac's hand, I felt his emotionally pained heart pounding in his chest. With each heartbeat and baited breath, we waited. Surrounded by our family and friends, this battle for normalcy and permanency would soon end for two precious boys who had experienced pain beyond imagination.

As the stern judge reached for his gavel and called the courtroom full of spectators to order, we knew the moment had arrived. For 18 months, we had been carrying the burden of fear. We were very accustomed to living every moment in fear that our two boys would be returned to the foster care system, or worse yet, be returned to those who had hurt them for so many years. With a single sentence uttered by the judge, we were about to find out if we were awarded the task of ensuring that these boys would never be hurt again.

We wished with every ounce of desperation to hear the verdict that we could deliver to Trent and Mike, who would be smiling from ear to ear despite their deep pain. Both Trent (age 9)and Mike (age 7) frequently smiled. This smile had become a permanent fixture, but it was nothing more than a masquerade. Their smiles served as a disguise to distract others from seeing the pain underneath the surface. It was a survival skill.

Because I, as their mother, had poured every ounce of my energy into learning and meeting their needs for the past 18 months, I was aware of the deep hurt and secrets that hid behind their smiles. I had a longing desire to hear the verdict that would be the start of a new hope. I hoped that those superficial smiles would soon be replaced with genuine and true happiness in knowing that they were loved and home!

As we anxiously awaited the verdict, my husband clutched my trembling hand by interlocking his fingers in mine. Over the years, his strong hand had become a source of strength for me. As I glanced down at our hands latched tightly together once again, I was suddenly flooded with memories of our life-long journey together. A journey that had culminated in that moment when we were waiting to hear if we were officially a family of four in the eyes of the law.

High School Sweethearts

My teenage heart fluttered every time he looked my way. I was only 17 at the time, but I felt like a princess every time he glanced in my direction. Despite the fact that I was a senior and he was merely a junior, every ounce of me was completely infatuated with this wonderful being who was caught somewhere between boy and man. I eagerly anticipated changing classes simply so I could catch a glimpse of his ashy blond hair and piercing blue eyes as I dashed to my locker that was located directly across the hall from his locker. Like most teenage girls experiencing their first crushes, my thoughts often wandered to daydreams of becoming the future wife of this boy I adored. Although I knew these visions were completely unlikely because we were still young, I fell prey to all of the fantasies of our potential life together. I often drifted off and planned our dream wedding and imagined our brick house surrounded by a white picket fence filled with deliriously happy and smiling children and a loyal dog that would greet us when we returned home each day.

A ski club trip to Wintergreen began the transformation of my fantasy into reality. Mac was an accomplished skier who glided gracefully down the toughest slopes with the ease of an olympic athlete. I, on the other hand, spent the entire trip attempting to remain upright and said a prayer before each trip down the mountain in hope of making it to the bottom without planting my face into the frigid snow. Mac frequently took time away from the expert hills to visit the beginner slopes in order to show off his abilities and gain my attention by throwing ice cold snow on me as he made rapid turns all around me during my feeble attempt to survive my trip down the hill of doom. Each time he sprayed me with snow, he glanced at me with a flirtatious smile and offered words of encouragement. This trip, that began with innocent flirting, set the stage for our life-long love story.

Over the next six years, our relationship grew strong. We became best friends and partners in all that we did. We spent countless hours laughing together, dreaming together, and simply enjoying being close to one another. I had no doubt that he was the man whom God had chosen for me.

As our relationship intensified, we began to discuss the possibility of the relationship lasting long term. Many hours were spent in detailed and heartfelt conversations about our future goals, morals, and how we felt God leading in our lives. Even prior to any discussion of marriage, we conversed for hours on end about children. Adoption became a frequent topic of conversation. Both Mac and I felt called at a very early age to create a family through adoption. While we both had a desire to have biological children, we agreed that adoption was going to be part of our future together. We connected very deeply on the issue and clearly understood that the Bible had called us to care for those in need. After 6 years of dating, prayers, and ensuring that our life goals coincided, Mac decided to take our lengthy relationship to the next level with a marriage proposal. I responded with an immediate yes.

After years of dreaming and planning, we started our lives together as a married couple with a dream wedding surrounded by our friends and family. While we planned to submit our lives to God and always follow His will, we had no idea what was in store for our future.

Life Sets In

As newlyweds, we were filled with hopeful thoughts, dreams for the future, and detailed plans. From an early age, I had proven to be a very organized. I had our lives planned out far in advance. The naivety of youth reinforced my belief that I could plan each step of life and that my plan would be carried out with ease.

Early in our marriage, my detailed plans came to fruition as planned, and I felt very much in control of life and my surroundings. I was able to check many of the items off of our list of goals. I became a licensed special education teacher after obtaining my Bachelor of Science in Early Childhood Special Education from the University of Maryland. Shortly after I received my degree, Mac completed his undergraduate degree from the University of Maryland in Animal Science and then obtained his Doctorate of Veterinary Medicine Degree from North Carolina State College of Veterinary Medicine. Every aspect of life was following my proposed timeline. Next on the agenda was to start a family.

Mac and I had a mutual commitment to having children and decided early on in our relationship that we would have our own biological children and would then expand our family through international adoption. I falsely assumed that I would be checking those items off of our list in a timely manner just like every other aspect of our life plan. I was ignorantly certain that my plan would come to pass with ease and we would make our family complete by the time we were 30 years old.

Years went by as we focused on success in our careers, purchased a new home, and plunged completely into our church lives. The one piece that was continually missing was children. Mac and I went on day by day, conveniently ignoring the fact that we had not gotten pregnant despite the fact that we had been married nearly 6 years. The lack of children became increasingly painful as time passed.

Each holiday served as a reminder of the void in our lives. The time came to revisit our plan and talk openly and honestly about our plans to create a family as we had always discussed. Clearly our goal to have biological children prior to adoption had not come to fruition. Rather than spending time determining medical reasons for our infertility, we mutually decided to move forward by creating a family through adoption. I had very brief moments of grief related to our inability to have biological children, but I was consistently overcome by a sense of undeniable peace. Mac and I both viewed it as a sign that we were intended to create our family solely through adoption. We decided to step out on a journey of faith that would forever change us.

Once the decision was made, my days and nights were quickly consumed by hours of research on the topic of adoption. I was a planner and felt the need to educate myself on the matter. Confusion set in as I began to consider the various possibilities including international adoption, private domestic adoption, and adoption through foster care. The more research I completed, the more confused I became at the various possibilities. We prayed that God would show us the way as we started down the path to adopt internationally. Doors quickly closed as adoptions were ceased in Guatemala and other countries that we considered.

Eventually, Mac convinced me to attend an information session about adopting through the foster care system. I was very reluctant and admittedly had many misconceptions about the children in foster care. My fear was elevated by extensive background in child development. Despite my hesitations, we attended a session through our local Department of Social Services. Although my fears remained, after gaining an understanding of the needs that were surrounding us right in our local community, we left with a feeling of certainty that this was our intended path.

With great enthusiasm, we selected a local agency and began frantically gathering documents, attending parenting classes, and completing all required meetings. Once we made our definitive decision, we were eager and ready to create our family.

I quickly learned that adopting through the foster care system was not a quick and easy process. My patience was tested frequently as I waited on overworked social workers to complete paperwork. The agency did the best they could, but I quickly learned that those working in the field were often overworked and underpaid. They truly had a heart for the children and families they were serving but were often unable to complete the needed steps according to my desired timeline. Over time, I began to view this is an opportunity for God to grow my patience. In addition, I began to realize that I had no control over the situation and had to sit back and trust in His timing.

I approached the mailbox each day in hope of finding a large envelope from the state delivering our official license to foster and adopt. I was overcome with extreme excitement when I flipped open the mailbox door and saw a large manilla envelope on top of a stack of bills. I knew that the contents of the long awaited document made us official licensed foster parents and that we were ready to begin searching for our child.

After lengthy discussion, we clearly specified that we would only accept one child under the age of five. We were also unwilling to take a child who was not yet legally free to be adopted. Lastly, we were unwilling to accept a child who had experienced sexual abuse simply because I felt unprepared. Despite our list of stipulations, God clearly decided that He had other plans.

Mountain Dew and Ho Ho's

Each time I swallowed, tears formed in the corners of my very exhausted eyes. I stared out the car window and watched the sun peak out from behind the tree line as we traveled nearly two hours away to an event called "A Day To Remember." Despite the fact that we were specifically seeking one child under the age of five, our adoption social worker encouraged us to attend any and all match events in order to gain an opportunity to network with other social workers.

Like all other adoption-related topics, I had studied up on match events and learned that these were events where licensed adoptive families were able to spend face-to-face time with children who were eligible and waiting to be adopted. I was very hesitant to waste my time attending any of these events because the attendees were typically older children or children who were difficult to place in adoptive homes for a variety of other reasons. Mac and I had set clear parameters regarding the child we were seeking. Finding a child under the age of five at a match event was highly unlikely.

Despite my arguments and evident hesitations, I agreed to attend the "Day To Remember" event. At least I could enjoy the day since it took place on a beautiful man-made lake. Spots were very limited for adoptive families, so we reserved our spot for this event nearly a month in advance.

Two days before the event, I noticed severe pain each time I swallowed. A trip to our local urgent care confirmed that I had developed a painful case of strep throat. Strep throat, coupled with the narrow-minded thought that the event would be a waste of time, prompted me to cancel our trip. I delivered Mac the news of my decision. He was disappointed but understood my reasoning.

I tossed and turned throughout the night. While I was restless due to illness, visions of meeting children awaiting adoption flitted through my mind. I had spent many hours viewing profiles and descriptions of waiting children. However, meeting them in person could give me a new perspective. These visions caused a deep emotional battle that robbed me of my sleep.

Once I realized that sleep was evading me, I quietly climbed out of bed and made my way to my favorite comfortable chair in my living room. I snuggled up with my purring cat, my laptop, and a steaming cup of chamomile tea. I scrolled through the adoption photo listings for North Carolina and closely examined picture after picture of children who had experienced tremendous pain and were awaiting the love of a forever family. Some of the children had smiles plastered on their faces, but the pain was evident in their eyes. As I closely examined each picture I prayed that the child would find the home he or she deserved. Scrolling through the photos, I was reminded of the abundance of children in foster care who were older, part of a sibling group, or had special needs. However, I did not see any profiles that matched our ignorantly set criteria. I felt deep emotion for the children I saw there, but repressed it in defense of our "adopting one child under the age of five" plan.

When I snuck back into bed at around 3:00 a.m., I woke Mac from his deep slumber long enough to tell him that I had changed my mind and we should attend the match event. I stretched the truth and told him that I was feeling better and wanted to make the trip. While strep throat remained, I felt as if I had to respond to the deep emotional pull that I was feeling. Mac agreed and reached over to set his alarm. I prayed for each of the hurting children whose pictures were haunting me as I drifted back to sleep.

After the alarm sounded at 6:00 a.m., I eagerly hopped into a cold shower in an attempt to wake myself up from my very brief sleep. I downed my antibiotic and some Advil with an intense cup of coffee and we headed out the door. Thoughts of uncertainty flooded my mind as we travelled. Mac was always very quiet, but he seemed very enthusiastic as he spoke about his eagerness to spend the day on the lake engaging in some of his favorite activities such as water skiing and wake-boarding. Mac was able to tell when looking at me that I was not feeling well, so he made me promise that I would not get in the water and that I would remain on the shore during the day. Appreciating his concern, I promised to comply with his loving advice.

After a two-hour trip down the dull highway, we pulled up a long gravel road that ended at a sparkling man-made lake surrounded by lush green grass. Since we arrived early, we remained in the car and watched the children as they eagerly left their cars. Nearly all were older teens who looked like they were being escorted to the event by their social workers. Watching from a distance, we observed the children as they each received a green wristband. My curiosity was peaked regarding the wristbands, but I knew the mystery would soon be solved. After we watched a few additional vehicles arrive, we decided to navigate our way to the registration table. Despite the strong emotions I had experienced the previous night, I was very skeptical and had minimal expectations as we headed off to start our day.

Social workers greeted us at the table and promptly attached yellow bands to our wrists, explaining that these bands marked us as potential adoptive parents. The children awaiting adoption were wearing green bands, and social workers were wearing blue. After receiving our identifying wristbands and agenda for the day, we were encouraged to start interacting with the children.

Mac and I glanced into a field occupied by teens. Some were engaging in activities such as Frisbee or football. Others were awkwardly sitting near the trees and clearly felt uncomfortable in this setting. Within a few short moments, we realized that many of these children had been to match events before this one. They obviously knew their purpose for attending and longingly spoke to potential adoptive families regarding their hopes and dreams. I overheard a conversation between two of the teens and I felt inner pain when I recognized one of them from the website that I had explored the previous night. Their words were emotionally difficult to hear. One teen spoke to his new friend and shared that this was his fifteenth match event and that he could not understand why no one had selected him. His words caused deep emotion for me, and I hoped that someone would connect with the hurting child. However, I selfishly remained focused on my mission to adopt one child under the age of five years old.

Before we had time to engage with any of the teens, a social worker took us by the hand and led us to a quiet area to talk. She shared information about a specific sibling group who was registered to attend the event. We had not previously met this social worker, but she had seen our preferences regarding age on our registration form. She confirmed my fear that young children did not attend the match events but explained that a sibling group of four children would be attending. The group included one girl who was ten years old and three boys who were ages six, eight, and thirteen. She thought that we might enjoy spending time with them. We agreed to the meeting and waited near the entrance for the group to arrive.

We eagerly waited on a sun-faded bench that overlooked the water, our thoughts filled with eager anticipation. A light tap on the shoulder and a warm smile from a social worker interrupted our daydreaming. She introduced herself and began telling us about the sibling group she had escorted to the event. The social worker, Genevieve, and her supervisor hesitantly shared that the group of children had a very significant abuse history and would need a very strong and well-prepared family to meet their extensive emotional needs. In addition, she implied some uncertainty in terms of the future placement of the children. She hinted that the sibling group would likely need to be placed in separate homes due to their abuse history.

As we talked with Genevieve, I saw a group of very excited children approach. Genevieve introduced each of the children to us. Samantha, the 10-year-old female with dark brown hair, bright eyes, and beautiful smile approached. She was followed closely by her two younger brothers. Eight-year-old Drew had amazingly bold, brown eyes, and a wide smile. He appeared eager to get in the water as he glanced at the various available activities. Scampering after his older brother was 6-year-old Brian. Although the time for eating was still far away, this little spitfire with bright, blue eyes bee-lined directly for the food table at record speed. The table was mounding with all sorts of snacks including Mountain Dew and Ho Ho's. With widened eyes, he plowed into the junk food that was awaiting. He began frantically tearing open the wrappers before the social workers were able to stop him. Last in line was 13-year-old Travis. He walked very slowly without straying far from the supervising social worker. I had never before seen a child appear so visibly sad and empty. He glanced up for only very fleeting moments; eye contact appeared uncomfortable for him. He lethargically wandered to the nearest tree, pulled his hood over his head, and leaned back in a clear refusal to participate.

After Genevieve finished the introductions, Mac quickly took the younger two boys by the hands and headed for the inviting water. My heart skipped a beat as I watched my husband grasp the hands of these two beautiful boys who had just walked into our lives.

Since I had promised Mac that I would not get in the water, I sat on the bench along the shore for a few minutes and talked with Samantha. She immediately shared her likes and dislikes. Samantha proceeded to tell me about her love for animals and asked if we had pets. She then fired many detailed questions about our home and our life. While the younger boys did not seem to know the purpose for this day at the lake, she obviously understood that she may find an adoptive family at this event. We watched her younger brothers laugh uncontrollably as Mac launched them high into the air and they landed with humongous splashes as they smacked the water. Thankfully, they were suited up with life jackets since they evidently had no idea how to swim. My heart was full as I watched Mac encourage the two boys as they accomplished tasks that seemed to be new for them. Mac hopped on the ski boat with them and cheered them on as they attempted to water ski. I was in awe as I watched these sweet children soak up every moment of undivided attention from this man that they had just met.

After hours in the water, the boys swam to shore and joined Samantha and me for lunch. As we talked and ate a much needed meal, the children reached out and grasped our hands, requested numerous hugs, and allowed us to help them with their food. I felt like we were sharing a few brief moments that felt like family. Mac and I frequently glanced at one another with a look of overwhelming love. No part of me had expected to have such strong feelings toward children I had just met. My strong emotions toward these beautiful children frightened me very deeply. I did not attend this event expecting to meet children who would impact me in such a powerful way.

As we ate our chicken sandwiches, Samantha asked very direct questions about our desire to adopt. My heart broke when she asked if we would consider adopting them and she wanted to know how quickly she could call us "Mom and Dad." Tears welled up as I forced my emotions aside and attempted to redirect the painful conversation. Looking back now, both Mac and I would have said yes to adopting them in that moment if it would have been possible.

As we finished our lunch, Mac walked over and engaged Travis who had been parked by the tree in silence since he arrived. Mac leaned against the tree next to the sullen teen and had a quiet and calming conversation. I glanced up a brief moment later and Mac miraculously had Travis up playing Frisbee and interacting with his younger brothers. He had somehow connected with him enough to gain his trust in that moment. The boys played Frisbee happily for the next 30 minutes while I sat and spoke with the social workers who would be placing this group of children into adoptive homes.

While they were not able to share much detail, they repeatedly stated that these children had experienced significant abuse and would need tremendous help and support. They were clearly emphasizing their needs in order to gauge my reaction. As the conversation progressed, they saw that I was not frightened by their comments. I also asked them a number of very detailed questions.

During our conversation, I saw them watch with amazement as Mac engaged the children in a laughter-filled game of Frisbee. The social workers were extremely impressed at his ability to connect, especially with Travis, who rarely interacted with others willingly. I had always been proud of my husband, but that was a moment that will remain forever etched in my mind.

As the conversation and Frisbee game continued, I noticed that Brian was running in circles at high rates of speed and falling to the ground while screaming and laughing. The large number of Ho-Hos and sodas that he had consumed had obviously caused an overabundance of caffeine and sugar. While it created a child that was overly active, I found it wonderful to see a child who had lived through such pain escape his reality for a few short hours.

The last activity for the day was a special devotional message for all participants. It was a very powerful message about how you must "get off the dock" to live life to the fullest. The event coordinators gave each of the children a t-shirt and a dog tag with Jeremiah 29:11 engraved on the back. Drew placed his dog tag proudly around his neck and grasped it tightly in one hand and held my hand in the other. I wanted that moment to last forever as I felt his tiny fingers grasp mine.

As I glanced at my watch, I knew that life-changing day was soon coming to an end. I knew that no matter what the outcome, our lives were forever changed by spending time with these children who were precious in our eyes. We enjoyed every single moment with them and had dreams of making this a permanent situation. Our plan of adopting one child under the age of five was no longer in existence after meeting this group.

I began to cry quietly as they headed into the bathroom to change into their clothes for their drive home. Having no idea what the future would hold for any of us was nearly too much to face in that moment. As we said our painful goodbyes, Drew looked out the window with his saddened brown eyes and said, "I hope you can adopt us." In that moment, I knew these children were meant to be ours.

As we drove home, Mac and I were silent as a result of emotional exhaustion. I had been so caught up in the events of the day that I forgot that I was still very sick. I leaned my throbbing head against the cool window and drifted off to sleep with a feeling of peace as I dreamed of our future family. I quietly prayed and thanked God for stirring something in me to attend the event that we almost skipped. Mac reached over and grabbed my exhausted hand. We both knew that our lives were about to change.

Ready or Not

Waiting has never been a strength of mine. I am admittedly very impatient, even when it comes to unimportant issues. Drew, Brian, Samantha, and Travis dominated our thoughts since we had met them at the match event two months earlier. Although the details began to fade, I grasped tightly to my memories of their smiles and warm hands as they held mine. With each passing day, my hope of seeing them again faded. I eagerly clicked on my inbox each morning and evening, hoping to see the magical words I deeply desired about the children who had left a permanent mark on my heart. Although I wanted to pray for a quick answer, I prayed daily for patience and faith in God's plan for our lives.

One evening after I scarfed down some left-over turkey and rice soup, I took a quick glance at my email before heading out to complete the weekly mundane task of grocery shopping. I completely froze when I saw the email from Genevieve, the social worker we had met at the match event. The email was titled, "Robinson Boys." I experienced both disbelief and fear. We had waited so long for news that I had a difficult time believing it was real. I was fearful to read the words of the email. Would the news be good news or would it sever our hopes of bringing these children into our home?

Mac was not home, but I did not delude myself into thinking that I could wait for two hours until he returned home. I took a deep breath and clicked open the email. It was concise and to the point. It stated simply that the placement team had met and decided that Mac and I would be a perfect fit for Drew and Brian. Current school pictures of Drew and Brian were attached to the email. I smiled as I clicked open the pictures one at a time and remembered our day together at the lake.

I was overflowing with emotion that I wanted to share with Mac, but I knew that I could not reach him. Due to my lack of patience, I knew that keeping the news to myself was impossible. I immediately called my parents to tell them the news. My mom and dad had longed to become grandparents for years, so they were extremely happy to hear about the possibility. They were eager to see the pictures of their potential grandchildren, so I immediately forwarded them. I heard my Mom's voice fill with happiness as she opened the pictures of Drew and Brian.

I paced the floor with agitation as I waited for Mac to return from his Jiu-Jitsu class. When I finally heard the front door open, I ran to him, grabbed his hand, and escorted him straight to the computer. I remained silent and sat back as he read the words. I watched for his reaction. After a few minutes passed, he very calmly turned to me and said, "See, I told you to have a little faith." His calm demeanor was quite aggravating in my moment of utter excitement, so I jokingly smacked his arm as we moved to the living room for further conversation. Although we both knew that we would accept the adoptive placement, we mutually agreed to pray and wait 24 hours before responding.

The whirlwind rushing through my mind stole my sleep that night, so I spent much time in prayer, asking God repeatedly to show us His path through this process. In the middle of the night, I reached for my very favorite devotional book that typically remained on my nightstand. This book was special to me because I had received it on my baptism day many years ago. It was well-used with pages that were bent and faded. I randomly flipped it open to page 158. As I read, I burst into tears of joy. The message in this specific devotion was about how children were like kites and needed parents to give them wind and help them fly. The message was abundantly clear and confirming. I immediately began to feel confident that we were, without question, following God's will for our lives.

As the sun began to peak through the bedroom blinds, I quickly moved to my computer to respond with a resounding yes. We expressed our eagerness to see the boys as soon as possible.

After sending the confirmation email, emotions ranging from sheer joy and happiness to a debilitating fear of the unknown continued to overwhelm me. Questions began to flood my mind like a tidal wave. We had only met the boys one time before we decided to make them a part of our family. Would we blend together well? Would Drew and Brian ever love me to the same degree that biological children love their parents? Would we be able to meet their needs? What would happen to Samantha and Travis?

I had devoted my life and career to child development and education, but I had very little practical experience in working with children who had experienced trauma. At that moment, I decided that I would educate myself as much as possible on any topic related to adopting an older child from foster care. My Amazon account soon overflowed with book purchases, and my own personal library of resources began to grow. Since transitions from foster to adoptive homes were typically slow, I relaxed, feeling confident that I had the time and ability to gain the knowledge I needed to parent these boys before they came to live with us. For many hours, I tried to imagine the possible scenarios of neglect and abuse that landed these boys in foster care. While we still had very few details of the abuse and neglect that they had experienced, we were willing and felt able to take on the challenge.

As we prepared for a slow transition into our home, our phones went crazy with texts, e-mails and phone calls as our exciting news spread like wildfire. Family and friends were eager to help us prepare our home and our hearts to accept the boys.

Juvenile pictures of pastel jungle animals greeted me as I entered the bedroom we had thoughtfully prepared for the child we had inaccurately envisioned in our minds. The room was filled with many loving and nurturing touches that were selected to welcome a single child under the age of five. The room was prepared with a crib full of warm blankets and more plush animals than any child should possess. As I glanced at this welcoming room we had prepared, I quickly realized how much work was ahead in order to transition this room to one that would be appropriate for a six-year-old boy. In addition, we needed a second bedroom for eight-year-old Drew. Our guest bedroom was covered in very feminine floral décor and fragile decorative items. We decided that this room should be transformed into Drew's bedroom. My thoughts raced with ideas about how to transform these two rooms to welcome Brian and Drew. I relaxed, reminding myself that I had plenty of time to carefully consider the ideas and implement the necessary changes.

Each time the phone rang, we hoped that Genevieve, the social worker, was calling to schedule a meeting with our boys and begin the slow transition into our forever family. When we received the much anticipated call, she shared her excitement about our continued interest in adopting the boys. She explained that the team had decided to place Samantha and Travis in different homes. While I was deeply saddened to hear about that decision, I understood the reasoning based on what I had learned about their abuse history.

Since the decision was made that Drew and Brian would join our family, we were all eager to move forward. We quickly scheduled a time for our next visit. We solidified plans to meet our boys in four days in their hometown which was almost four hours away from our house.

The scheduled day could not come soon enough. I was like a child who was waiting to open presents on Christmas morning. When they day of our meeting finally arrived, I eagerly hopped into the car for the trip to see our boys for the second time.

As I talked incessantly during the entire drive, Mac had obviously tuned out my barrage of questions, concerns, comments, and repeated statements. Mac and I dealt with emotion very differently. He enjoyed remaining silent and escaped into his music as a distraction. I, however, wanted to talk. My most immediate and predominant fear was that the boys would not remember us. We had not seen them for two months. Many different scenarios of our reunion played through my mind. Each time, it ended with a sense of awkward discomfort. Finally, we approached the city limits. We were within fifteen minutes of being reunited with the boys who had stolen my heart.

I felt nauseous as we pulled our vehicle into the packed parking lot of a local bookstore. While the people scurrying in and out of the store were experiencing a typical day, this day was far from typical for us. We were doing something brand new; we were spending time with the children who would potentially complete our family unit. I felt a rush of emotions ranging from utter terror to hopefulness and indescribable joy. My heart started to pound at a rapid pace as I watched the minutes tick down on the clock in the car. As always, Mac sat calmly and leaned his head back to rest. I never understood how he was able to remain so calm in moments when I felt like I was going to explode. Similar to his response after receiving Genevieve's email, he looked at me and said, "Have a little faith, Baby; things will turn out the way they are meant to be." His sense of peace and calm was annoying, so I simply tuned him out and entered my realm of anxious thoughts yet again.

I glanced out the driver's side window and saw a vehicle pull into the space next to ours. I recognized the welcoming face of Genevieve and spotted two little heads peering out the window in the back seat. Both boys had piercing and beautiful eyes that glanced our way with a loving smile. That glance alleviated all of my fear that they had forgotten us. They were obviously eager to free themselves from the constraints of their seatbelts and get out of the car to greet us. My heart was pounding as I opened the car door. Before I could get around the back bumper, Drew ran at full speed and climbed Mac like a tree. He wrapped his little legs around Mac's body and said, "I missed you." Brian followed shortly behind Drew and approached us for welcoming hugs. In that instant, all my worries melted away, and I was able to focus on our exciting day ahead.

We followed Genevieve to a local park. She spoke with us briefly and drove away to leave us for the day with two very excited and extremely active little boys. Watching her pull away was very surreal. I realized that we would soon feel what it was like to function as a family of four.

The park had a very intricate, wooden climbing structure with slides, bridges, hidden tunnels, and other secret passages. The boys immediately engaged us in an imaginary game of Castle. The roles were immediately assigned: Mac was the king, I was the queen, and the boys were the knights who had the job of protecting us from the giant evil dragons that lurked in the mist. Nothing else existed in those moments as we ran, hid, climbed, and defeated the dragon as a team. The sweat-covered knights continually came to check on me, their queen, to make sure I was safe. I vividly recall watching them from my "tower" and almost bursting into a flood of tears. They appeared so happy, but I knew that significant pain was lying behind their smiles and laughter. They were on their absolute best behavior and frequently used ideal manners that had obviously been drilled and memorized. The temperature climbed, and we all began to get overheated. As a result we decided to put an end to our game of Castle and move to the next activity. I reveled in the simple moment when I provided them with water to quench their thirst and grabbed their sweaty little hands to lead them safely to the car; I felt like a mom!

The boys talked ceaselessly as we drove to our next location. We arrived at a nearby bowling alley within a few short minutes. The boys both quieted as we approached the venue. With a look of embarrassment on his vulnerable little face, Drew explained that they had never been bowling. Mac chimed in and very calmly stated, "Well, we will teach you." That reassuring statement seemed to provide a sense of relief for them as we entered the bowling ally that smelled of old gym socks.

We spent the next two hours engaging in what is still the most entertaining game of bowling I have ever played. At one point, Brian bowled the ball backwards, away from the lane. As soon as we realized that no one was injured by the flying seven-pound ball of fury, we all laughed until our insides hurt. In addition to bowling the ball backwards, Brian also somehow discovered an innovative way to launch the ball into the neighboring lane that was to the right of our assigned location.

While the two angels were obviously trying to maintain their best behavior, we noticed that they were getting tired as the day progressed. Despite the fact that they were likely emotionally exhausted, their activity levels increased. They seemed to be moving faster to keep themselves alert so that they did not miss a moment. We also saw fear and anxiety creeping through their facades of happiness. Drew began questioning us about the time and asked how many hours we had remaining together. When we explained that we were going to get some dinner and then our visit was over, he looked clearly distressed and wiped a tear from his sweat-drenched body. Throughout the day, I had learned that Drew craved physical affection; he had approached us often for hugs of reassurance. So I reached over and grabbed his little, shaking hand in an effort to provide comfort.

The smell of steak wafted through the air as we exited the car in the parking lot of a well-known steakhouse. We wanted to treat the boys to a good meal after an activity-filled day. As we approached the door, Drew said, "I have never been to a big restaurant like this." When asked what restaurants they liked, both boys stated that they had only been to fast food establishments. We quickly realized that this would be another new experience for them. With joy, I told the hostess we needed seating for a family of four. I felt a jolt of satisfaction when those words left my lips.

As we sat, little hands immediately reached for the steaming rolls that were waiting in the basket in the middle of the round table. While we knew we were not their legal parents, we felt the need to teach some table manners that had evidently been overlooked in the past. We demonstrated proper placement of the cloth napkin in your lap and asked them to wait patiently before grabbing food. Both Drew and Brian appeared completely overwhelmed at the thought of making a selection from the menu. In order to alleviate the uncertainty, we ordered a steak for each of them from the kids menu.

As we waited for our meal to arrive, we asked the boys if we could pray. Without hesitation, Drew offered to say the prayer. I was shocked to see an 8-year-old boy, who had such a traumatic upbringing, so eager and willing to pray publicly. My arms were covered in goosebumps as he offered a very adult-like prayer, thanking God for the day we had together and for the food we were about to eat. Mac and I glanced at each other with a look of contentment. We had no question that this was our family!

We watched in utter disbelief as the boys consumed enough food to feed multiple grown men. They requested salad, mushrooms, onions and other foods that children typically reject.

Drew repeatedly checked Mac's watch since he knew our visit would soon be coming to an end. He appeared to be stalling by eating every crumb he could locate on the table. Drew began asking questions about when we would see them again and became visibly anxious when we received the bill. In his fragile mind, the check was an indication that our time together was nearly over. I so desperately wanted to grab them in my arms and take them home with us in that moment. However, I knew that was not an option, and I needed to be very careful with my verbal message in order to keep from providing false hope. We still had many details to work out regarding timing, placement and their transition into our home.

Extreme sadness approached as we sat in the parking lot to meet Genevieve who would return the boys to a foster home filled with uncertainty and fear. Thinking about them leaving pained me deeply. Genevieve pulled up and asked if she could speak to us privately. We took a brief walk. Before she had a chance to ask how the visit had gone, I looked her directly and said, "We want to bring them home to us as soon as possible." She let out a huge sigh of relief and shared that she needed to get them out of their current placement as soon as possible due to some concerns that she could not share. Then she also explained that the boys were not legally free to be adopted. That terminology was somewhat unfamiliar, so I asked questions to clarify. It meant that the Termination of Parental Rights Hearing had not yet happened and that the case had the potential of taking a little longer than anticipated. We were assured that adoption would be the end result, but we would need to be patient.

We had already connected with the boys that we knew were meant to be ours. No words or warnings could have caused us to change our minds at that point. Mac and I explained that we were willing to wait for the court process as long as everyone was certain that adoption would be the end result. We had been foster parents for many previous years, but this time we were strictly interested in becoming adoptive parents. My heart was simply too fragile to even consider the possibility of losing these children who I had grown to love in a way I never imagined in such a short time. We accepted this complication without hesitation and asked when the boys could move into our home. We had planned for a slow transition period, but soon discovered that our boys would be coming home in one week!

Frantic preparations began as we called in our troop of friends and family to assist in transforming the rooms that I thought I had months to prepare. Neighbors came and helped assemble bookshelves and new beds. Friends, family, and church members all assisted with the collection of toys, clothing, books, and other necessities. The floral guest bedroom was quickly transformed into a G.I. Joe-themed headquarters. At the same time, our jungle-themed baby room was transformed into a rainforest paradise for a six-year-old. After the room transformations were completed, we began to focus on preparing our hearts and minds for the arrival that was going to change our lives forever.

Excitement took hold and I often found myself getting caught up in the overwhelming joy of creating a family. Despite my overeager happiness, I attempted to grasp the reality that this transition was going to be another move for these boys who had already experienced four previous relocations. I had to face a harsh reality. While this adoption would make Mac and I extremely happy, the boys were already facing deep pain and loss. I frequently prayed, asking God to prepare my heart for the coming trials.

Coming Home

Walking up and down the aisle at the grocery store was exhausting. I paced the aisles enough times to have considered it a workout for the day. I glanced at the unending food choices and did my best to anticipate what Drew and Brian would eat once they arrived. In less than six hours, two boys were joining our family forever, and I did not even know what they liked to eat. Our steakhouse excursion proved to me that they were not picky eaters. However, I wanted to do my best to provide a variety of child-friendly foods to welcome them when they arrived.

I finally settled on making a pot of chicken tortilla soup for the adults and macaroni and cheese for the boys. I felt certain that was a safe choice. Macaroni and cheese was a comfort food, and I aimed to make them feel comfortable from the second the entered our home.

The house was clean, the rooms were prepared, and the food was waiting. All that was missing was the arrival of Brian and Drew. Genevieve sent a text to inform us that they were running behind schedule due to an issue with the car seat. The thought of passing additional time was simply torturous.

I wondered what the boys were thinking as they pulled away from their foster home for the final time. They were about to move to a home they had never seen with two people they had met only twice. While I was fantasizing about them being extremely excited and overly joyous, I knew the reality was more likely that they were filled with fear of the unknown. I piddled around in the kitchen and swept the floor for the eighth time to pass the dragging time. Mac eventually got the text saying that they were 10 minutes away. I took a deep breath and walked to the bedroom to offer a silent prayer, asking God to guide every step of this journey. Feeling completely and totally powerless and unprepared in that moment, I turned our adoption journey over to Him.

I heard the car door slam, so I eagerly walked to the front door to welcome the boys to their forever home. I was ecstatic to see their beautiful faces again. They both looked up in awe at the outside of the house and stated that they had never seen such a big house. They were each clutching a tattered duffle bag and a trash bag. Later we discovered that the trash bag was filled with broken Happy Meal toys and trash. The social worker also carried in one set of plastic drawers that appeared to be full of broken toys and trash. I assumed that we would need to make multiple trips to the car to bring in their personal belongings but soon realized that the bags and drawers contained everything they owned. I felt sickened to think that these boys had moved from a home and had nothing but a torn bag full of stained clothing that no longer fit and a trash bag filled with broken toys that came free with junk food meals. My research and training had warned that this was often the case, but to see it first hand was life changing. They barged through the front door and gripped their bag of pathetic belongings, clearly not wanting to let go of their few personal possessions. I allowed them to carry the bags while we showed them around the house.

We toured every room on the first floor. They glanced around their new home with obvious trepidation. They were overly interested in the kitchen and seemed relieved to see that we had an abundance of food available. Brian wanted me to open the refrigerator to show him the food inside, so I happily obliged.

After completing our tour of the first story, we moved upstairs and showed each of them their rooms. They were very touched by the fact that we remembered their interest and decorated their rooms accordingly. Each room was packed full of new toys, games, clothing, and other personal items. They were obviously overstimulated by the amount of material items we had provided. Reading their behavioral cues, I began to rapidly stash some of the items in the closet as they walked out.

We moved back downstairs as a family and enjoyed our first meal together in our home. To my surprise, both boys wanted to eat the Chicken Tortilla Soup and salad instead of the macaroni and cheese. Drew said that he wanted to eat the soup because I had made it myself.

When their little bellies were sufficiently full, we moved to the couch to talk about our family rules. Genevieve took this as her cue to depart and allowed us begin our new life together as a family of four. We embraced her with a big hug of thanks and scheduled a time to follow up within the next few days. Genevieve was a compassionate and caring social worker who deeply cared about Drew and Brian. We felt very fortunate to have her in our lives.

After a few moments of discussion, I witnessed some incessant yawning and decided to begin the bedtime process. I was a bundle of nerves not knowing what to expect. I kept thinking that I was being selfish for being nervous. These two little children had experienced so much trauma in their past and had no idea if we could be trusted. They had no idea if they were safe in their new and overwhelming environment. I knew that they were likely filled with tremendous fear and anxiety. I so desperately wanted them to know that they would never be hurt again. Words were meaningless: we would have to prove that to them over time.

We headed up the long flight of stairs and sat by Brian on his bed that was decorated to his liking. We turned on his nightlight and read him two bedtime stories. He appeared very peaceful and content and easily drifted off to sleep while we remained in the room. He was younger and was simply utterly exhausted.

We crossed into Drew's room and saw a very different scenario. He was clearly agitated and appeared very fearful so we quickly turned on his nightlight and his bathroom light. He climbed into bed willingly, but tucked himself deeply under the covers to the point of barely being able to breathe. Assuming he was bundled up in order to stay warm we asked him if we should turn off his fan. He quickly said no and with a shaky voice stated, "I'm scared." I reached for his hand to sooth him, but before the words left my mouth, Mac dropped down on the floor in order to be on eye level with the frightened little boy and began to sing the "Marine Corps Hymn" in a very off-tune key. I had been married to Mac for over 12 years and had never heard him sing. It was horribly off key, but every note of it was from his heart. Drew immediately calmed at the sound of his voice. His breathing slowed and his eyes began to close.

I was more in love with my husband during that moment than I had ever been in the past. Mac had always carried himself with a tough and strong demeanor and was frequently mistaken for a police officer or a military officer. However, in that moment, he made himself completely vulnerable for the sake of a child in need. I cried as I watched Drew drift off to sleep, thanks to Mac's selfless efforts. Exhausted from the emotion, we headed to bed. Our new life had begun.

The Honeymoon Is Over

The maternal side of me always dreamed of picnics in the park, picking out adorable outfits for my kids to wear, sharing funny stories with other parents, and leading a blissfully peaceful life. The first few weeks were filled with magical moments and memories as we learned to live life as a family unit.

My training warred with the maternal side of me that was emerging. I knew from my background in psychology that this joyous honeymoon period would end at some point. My assumptions were correct. We quickly realized that because we had created our family in a non-traditional manner, our path would look very different from other families we knew. When these children entered our lives for the first time at the ages of six and eight, we had already lost some very significant years of bonding and parenting. Because of my background in child development, I was painfully aware of the importance of the early years and the long lasting implications of neglect and trauma on brain development and behavior. While I loved Brian and Drew with every bit of my being, the realization that parenting them would be all consuming quickly overwhelmed me. While I did not want to admit it, I was not surprised to learn that their environmental instability had caused significant delays and behavioral issues.

I spent the next month navigating through the needs of these two boys who had been neglected and abused for many years. I often felt incompetent, both as a parent and a professional who specialized in child development and behavior management. My training with traditional behavior management methods were obviously ineffective with them. Their responses were different from the responses of the children I had taught in the schools for many years. I quickly realized that I needed further education and training in the area of children who had experienced trauma. Because their needs were so significant, we were forced to become detectives, digging into their trauma in order to identify reasons behind specific behaviors and reactions. One of the tools that I used in this investigation was a detailed daily journal that I began on the night of their arrival.

While we spent every day thanking God for bringing our boys home, we quickly realized that the road to healing would be long. Years of extreme neglect, domestic violence, and other forms of abuse had landed these boys in foster care. While the boys were not at fault for the abuse, it could not be healed overnight. We now had the job of helping them pick up and put together the pieces of their shattered lives. In spite of the challenges that were ahead of us, I felt truly honored that Mac and I were the ones who had been chosen to help them navigate through their tremendous pain. We knew that the only way to gain true healing would be to gain further knowledge in the area of trauma and to lead them to the ultimate healer: God.

The insight into the reality of their needs caused me to mourn some of the idealistic fantasies that I had created in my mind. After opening my heart and my home to children who had been hurt very deeply by others, I so desperately wanted to believe that unconditional love would serve as the magic quick fix. Despite the insights that I knew, I continued to find myself slipping into that fantasy, but the pain that surfaced frequently for the boys served as reality checks to destroy that fantasy.

Mac and I vowed to travel the healing journey by their sides. We knew the journey would be painful and exhausting. I have never been fearful of physical pain. Physical pain is what makes me know that I am alive. What has always haunted me has been emotional pain that can be hidden behind a smile or false look of contentment. Brian and Drew had experienced such deep and damaging pain, but they had mastered the ability to keep a smile on their faces in order to please those around them. The time had come to see what was haunting them behind their smiles.

What's In A Name?

Awkward moments frequently occurred during the first few weeks of being together as a new family. When Drew and Brian arrived in our home, the placement was considered "foster to adopt." When we learned that the case could be tied up in court for a lengthy period of time, the uncertainty of permanency lingered. While we were told with certainty that adoption was the plan, we did not want to promise the boys that they would remain with us forever until the parental rights of the birth family were officially terminated in court.

We told Drew and Brian upon entering our home that they could call us whatever made them feel comfortable. Since they had previously traveled through multiple foster homes, they decided to call us Mrs. Pam and Mr. Mac which is how they referred to adults in previous placements. We knew in our hearts that this placement was unlike the others from their past, but we also understood that they needed significant time to grasp the reality of a permanent home. They had spent their early years filled with uncertainty and an inability to trust adults. With each move, that lack of certainty and trust grew stronger. They had no reason to trust us until we proved to them that we were different from the other adults who had failed them.

Emotions were very raw as the honeymoon period began to subside. Fear and anxiety began to rule their hearts as the initial shock of another move faded. Anxiety was building each day, and I noted behavioral changes. For instance, Drew incessantly picked his lips, and Brian bit his fingers to the point of bleeding. I also saw a significant amount of rocking and other self-soothing behaviors.

One afternoon as Drew wrote and drew pictures in his journal, he began to cry. Since I had learned that he was extremely affectionate, I reached for his hand and began to rub it. It was evident that it soothed him as his breathing slowed, but he remained agitated. Before I could even ask about the tears, he looked me in the eyes and said, "I want to call you Mom, but I'm afraid the adoption won't happen." I took a long, thoughtful pause before responding to him. I was stunned by his awareness of the situation; he was obviously more aware of the potential complications than I had anticipated. He understood that his placement in our home was not yet permanent. Forming a response was difficult. I finally reminded him that adoption was the plan but that we would need to be patient while we waited. When tears began to roll down my cheeks, he reached up and gently wiped away my tear and said, "So can I call you Mom and Dad anyway?" I held him tight and confirmed that he could call us whatever felt comfortable for him.

Many adoptive parents long for the day that the children address them as Mom and Dad. I knew the realization that another woman gave birth to them would always be present and respected. However, the woman who gave birth to them had been unable to do her job. I now had the job of feeding them, keeping them safe, teaching them, and showing them each and every day that they were loved and precious to us. To be called Mom felt like a true honor and a right of passage. I had been their mom in my heart from the day they entered my life. From that day forward we were no longer Mrs. Pam and Mr. Mac; we were Mom and Dad.

Starting to Heal

The golden leaves began falling from the trees, and the weather began to cool as we entered autumn. Brian and Drew began to feel comfortable in their new home, and we settled into our routines that included regular therapy sessions, monthly visits from multiple social workers and guardian's ad litem, and typical daily activities such as homework and time together as a family. We had not received any additional information about the progression of the courts, and we chose not to ask too many questions in order to keep our anxiety at a dull roar.

As the boys' comfort levels increased, so did their willingness to express any and all emotions. We had proven ourselves to be safe, and Drew developed a confidence in our ability to remain non-judgmental about his past trauma. Sadness and anger became regular emotions that he demonstrated as he shared detailed stories of his experiences. While Brian did not show as many emotions as Drew, both of the boys shared detailed stories of extreme neglect and domestic violence that they witnessed almost daily during their early years. The abuse was extensive and had hurt them so deeply that I often wondered if we would ever successfully navigate the pain ahead. As they disclosed this abuse, I remained as supportive as possible and was very careful not to influence thoughts or feelings. Mac and I always spoke positively about their birth parents in an attempt to ease the pain. We wanted the healing process to belong to them and to be completed in their own timing and manner. Freedom from their past seemed to come with each story they shared.

Drew expressed his emotions very freely, but Brian remained very quiet and rarely showed emotion of any sort. Even when a memory should have caused tremendous emotional pain, he kept a false smile plastered on his angelic face. Not only did he lack emotion while expressing painful memories, he did not exhibit emotion even when hurt physically.

One day, Brian fell off his bike onto the concrete with a crash. He cut his knee and blood flowed down his tiny leg. I expected the typical scenario with a tearful child approaching his mom for comfort, a Band-aid, and a healing kiss. Instead, he stood up from his crash with a look of pain, but he did not allow any tears to flow. He sought no comfort from those around him. I watched him in awe. In that moment, I realized that he had learned at an early age that emotion was completely ineffective in gaining a response from the adults around him. When I checked on him to make sure he was not injured and saw the look of pain on his face, I gave him permission to cry if he was hurt, but he remained stoic. His inability to express his pain through tears was difficult to watch. I realized that this was just one of the results of past neglect. Neglect in early childhood years sends a message to the child that he is not important. In some ways abuse is easier to experience than neglect. When a child is abused, they at least feel like they exist; when they are neglected, their existence is not even recognized. Obviously, Brian had learned that he was not worthy of a response when he showed emotion. As a result, he had taught himself to completely turn off emotions. Despite his lack of emotion, I held him as I cleaned and bandaged his wound. I explained to him that my job as his mom was to keep him safe and to help him when he needed help. He looked at me with a very puzzled look and returned to playing.

Tears flowed from my tired eyes nightly as I recorded my thoughts and observations in my journal. Each day seemed to reveal additional pain as the boys began to realize how a family was supposed to function. Their past seemed to become more painful as they realized what they had missed. I was fully prepared and expected to hear comments about a desire to see their birth parents, but those words were never spoken. Instead, we began to hear frequent comments from both boys about their desire to be adopted and remain with us forever. We had been assured that adoption was the plan, so we confidently told them that we simply had to wait.

Filling the Holes

Brian and Drew had spent the first years of their life focused on making sure that their basic safety needs were met and that they had food to eat. They also lived in constant fear of moving to yet another home. As a result, they could not focus on their development. Even if they would have had the time and energy to focus on that development, many basic skills were never taught. We quickly discovered and began to fill these holes in their development. We taught manners, basic hygiene, proper play skills, social skills, and stress management techniques. Very frequently, we discovered missing skills during behavioral meltdowns.

One of these meltdowns happened on a Sunday morning. Drew sat on the steps as we prepared to go to church. Since arriving he had always dressed himself independently and was able to put on his shoes without difficulty. That morning, he asked me to tie his shoes. I assumed this request was an attention-seeking behavior because he had been tying his shoes independently since arriving. In order to promote continued independence, I asked him to tie them on his own. His face reddened and he began to get visibly angry. I proceeded to tell him that we would be leaving in five minutes and that he needed to get his shoes on his feet. I knew we had a mounting behavior problem since he was staring blankly at the floor. I issued one more warning, and he proceeded to turn around and stomp up the steps to his room. Having no idea what was provoking the behavior, I entered his room nearly five minutes later and found him in the corner in a flood of tears. He looked up at my frustrated face and yelled, "I can't tie them; no one ever taught me!" Confused by his response, I looked at him in disbelief. I was confused since he had been managing his shoes since he arrived. He then explained that he had been slipping his his feet into his shoes every day but was unable to do that with the dress shoes I had purchased the previous day. I felt such a sense of sadness as I realized that he had been afraid to ask for help with a task that he felt he should have mastered many years ago. I apologized for the misunderstanding and held him as he cried. I assured him that we would teach him to tie his shoes in the immediate future. Moments like these were frequent and painful for both boys. We discovered many missing skills in this manner over time. Each time, we taught them the needed skill and focused on building their very fragile self esteem.

In addition to missing skills, we also soon realized that nearly every experience was new for Brian and Drew. They obviously had not been exposed to activities that most children take for granted; each experience seemed new and frightening for them. They had never been to the beach, ridden a train, taken a plane ride, gone to museums, or tried a variety of foods. We often prompted exposure to new events and activities. They conquered many fears and felt stronger with each new experience.

While I was thankful that we were able to share so many firsts with them, I was also very saddened by the fact that they had such limited exposure to the world as children. I vowed to change that as we planned day trips, special events, and family vacations. The time

had come to show them the world
around them.

Bologna and Ketchup Sandwiches

Mounds of wrappers and trash from various food items hidden behind Brian's bed glared at me as I cleaned. His face filled with shame as he pulled out cracker wrappers, sugar packets, rotting fruit, and packets of half-eaten Crystal Light drink powder. My initial reaction was anger. I had fed him wonderful, home-cooked meals since the day he entered our home; he had never once gone hungry under our roof. I was deeply hurt when I realized that he still did not trust us to meet his basic needs.

When entering the process of adoption, I knew that food issues were prevalent among children who had spent time in foster care. However, I was not prepared for these emotions that the food issues evoked. In the midst of my anger, I paused to consider how truly frightened and anxious Brian must have felt in order to hide food in his room to make sure he would have something to eat. Brian often talked about how they had lacked food when they lived with their birth family. Shortly after his arrival to our house, we had begun closely monitoring his food intake. Without this close monitoring, he often ate to the point of becoming sick. I often faced harsh comments from other people who did not understand the reasons that we limited and monitored his food. As I realized that the mounds of food were created by his fear of not having enough to eat, my anger quickly changed to sadness. I pulled him close to me and held him while reassuring him that he would never go hungry again.

Although food issues were not as prominent with Drew, he often told stories of going hungry and searching for food. He shared a very detailed memory of climbing on the stove in order to reach a bottle of syrup that was in a high cabinet. He described that as being the best syrup he ever tasted after feeling hunger pangs in his little belly from lack of nourishment.

Both boys were willing to eat almost anything I prepared, and they were amazed that I took the time to cook for them each day. Although they qualified for free lunch at school since they were technically in foster care, they requested that I pack their lunches. They seemed to be comforted by this simple act; it showed them that I cared enough to take the time to complete this task for them. So I carefully packed their lunches each night with a healthy meal and wrote a special note on a napkin that I lovingly placed on top of the food.

One day after school, I walked into Drew's room and saw him reading through the notes on the napkins he had saved. Since he did not see me approaching, I was able to observe him quietly reading the notes as tears flowed down his reddened face. As I entered the room, he looked at me and said, "My birth mom cooked for me one time." Although I was completely disheartened by the realization that his birth mother had only cooked for him once, I wanted to help this become a good and valuable memory for him. I asked him to tell me about his one and only memorable meal. He explained that she had warmed up a bag of peas. I waited for more details about the meal that stood out so prominently in his memories, but none followed. The peas were the only meal that he could remember his birth mother preparing for him. Biting my tongue I said, "Wow, I bet those were good, weren't they?" He then climbed into my lap and grasped onto me with a firm hold and began weeping uncontrollably and thanking me for taking the time to feed him. I could not muster any words in that moment; I simply wept with him.

Once Drew calmed his emotions, he went on to tell me that his sister, Samantha, often located food for them to eat and that she had mastered the making of bologna and ketchup sandwiches. Although he did not like the taste, he said that at least he did not go hungry when she made those horrible sandwiches. He described in vivid detail how his stomach would hurt from sheer emptiness. I was heartbroken and promised him that he would never go hungry again. He simply wrapped his arms around my neck and gripped me for a nurturing hug. In those moments, I felt as if I was drowning. I found it difficult to keep the pain from their past from consuming me.

We had so much pain and trauma to overcome. As we waded through the pain-filled days, my prayers were often fleeting thoughts that were from a place of sheer desperation, such as "God, please help us!"

No More Secrets

Secrets have the ability to destroy people. As children who had learned from an early age that adults were not safe, Brian and Drew held many skeletons in their tiny closets that needed to be revealed in order to begin healing. In our home, they felt safe for the first time in their lives. As feelings of safety increased, they began dropping hints about various forms of abuse they had endured in order to gauge our reaction. Each and every time they disclosed information, we responded in a supportive and loving manner and ensured them it was no fault of their own. Neglect and domestic violence had been a very prominent demon in their past, but we suspected that even deeper hurt was present.

As a family, we established a daily check-in time to discuss our thoughts and emotions. Those conversations typically took place prior to being tucked into bed at night. Since he was older, the conversations with Drew became very detailed and filled with emotion. From an early age, he demonstrated extremely high emotional intelligence and was keenly aware that he needed to talk about his past trauma in order to move beyond the pain. He willingly faced his trauma head on. He had an irresistible urge to fiddle with objects, rip items, or find an alternate way to keep his hands occupied when talking about difficult subjects. It served as a distraction from the painful words that flowed from his lips. He accidentally ruined many of my shirts by obsessively plucking beads or decorative sequins from them while exposing his deepest secrets. Our nightly conversations intensified over time as he tested the waters to ensure my loyalty and ability to handle the details that he needed to share.

One evening at tuck-in time, Drew's head was buried deep into his pillow as he began to talk. His arms were covered in hives, and he refused to look me in the face. He uttered words that broke me. He said, "Mom, I want to tell you something, but you will never love me again." I sat on the floor, grabbed his hand tightly and reassured him as I had so many times in the past. He started uttering very self-deprecating comments, such as "I am so ugly. No one can love me. I am so stupid. You are going to hate me." His voice escalated and the tension mounted. I knew he was preparing to expose his darkest secrets. I wanted to be certain that I handled it properly, so I said a quick prayer in my head and began to calm him by gently rubbing his hand. He clasped my hand so tightly that I thought my fingers were going to snap under his grip. He shouted, "I wish you gave birth to me and none of this would have happened." I sat calmly and waited for him to expose his inner demons. He continued to squirm uncontrollably and buried his head deep into the pillows as he exposed his darkest secrets that he had never shared with anyone.

Drew revealed extensive sexual abuse that he suffered between the ages of 3-7 at the hands of his uncle and his brother, Travis. He was so consumed by guilt and shame that he would not make eye contact and simply hid under every pillow and blanket he could find. I held him for what seemed like hours and rocked him repeating the words he needed to hear: "It's not your fault." He eventually calmed emotionally, looked me in the face, and said, "How can you still love me?". Heartbroken, I assured him that nothing could ever change that truth and we would help him heal from this hurt.

With this disclosure, I felt certain that the trauma had become insurmountable. I felt physically sickened as I considered all that Drew and Brian had faced in their young lives.

Feeling completely unprepared, I immediately began reading, taking classes and learning everything possible about helping children overcome sexual abuse. A huge weight seemed to be lifted from Drew when he realized that I was not judging him and that he no longer needed to carry the painful secrets alone. I assured him daily that we would fight the battle as a family with God in the lead.

We spent significant time working through the newly exposed abuse in therapy and at home. We had Drew evaluated. The evaluation confirmed that he had been sexually victimized, but he was not at risk for acting out sexually toward other children. We spent considerable time reteaching sexuality so that he could understand the biblical definition and would develop a clear and healthy sexual relationship with his spouse in the future.

In addition to Drew's disclosure about sexual abuse, Brian disclosed physical abuse that he vividly recalled suffering at the hands of Lilith, the maternal grandmother. He had very detailed memories of being thrown into a wall when he would not stop crying. He did not have an extensive vocabulary, but he described the pain and fear to the best of his ability. He was visibly fearful when describing the incident. I had enough training in psychology to know that the level of fear he displayed was an indication of active Post Traumatic Stress Disorder.

Each time either of the boys disclosed more details about their abuse, I broke on the inside while attempting to react with minimal emotion. Many nights, I left their rooms after hearing horrific details and quickly moved to my closet and dropped to the floor and cried as I thought of the physical and emotional pain they had endured. My closet became my hiding place. I often stepped in there when overcome by emotion. I vowed to never let them be hurt again.

A Ripple In The Water

Eating meals on the back porch
became a favorite activity for our family
during the summer months. As
temperatures began to drop in the fall,
we did not want to give it up. Jeans and
hoodies replaced the summer shorts.
We were all gathered in that familiar
spot when we received the call that
caused the ripple.

Mac had just taken a bite of his
chicken when he received a phone call.
After looking at his phone to identify the
caller, he quickly wiped his mouth and
walked inside to answer the call. Mac
typically did not answer phone calls
during dinner, so I knew that it must
have been something he viewed as
important. After answering the phone,
he quickly moved to our bedroom and
closed the door. His actions concerned
me, so I asked the boys to remain
outside on the porch while I joined Mac
in the bedroom.

As I entered the bedroom, I saw the
unsettled look on Mac's face and heard
his serious conversation with the
guardian ad litem. As far as we knew,
everything was proceeding as intended

in the court system to move toward terminating the parental rights of the birth parents. However, the guardian ad litem shared news that caused me to feel sick to my stomach. He explained that the courts had attempted to cut the parental rights after more than five years of interactions with the Department of Social Services (DSS). The parents reacted by hiring a private attorney to advocate on their behalf. He warned us to prepare for a lengthy battle in court.

Mac directly asked the question, "Is there a chance they could end up back in foster care or return to their birth family?" The answer was one that was like a knife to my stomach. After reassuring us that he felt, without question, that they should remain with us, he said, "Yes, there is a chance." I felt like I could no longer breath in that moment. My entire world came crashing down with one phone call. I would have kept my heart locked up tight from the start if I had any indication that the boys would not remain with us forever. Now I could not protect my heart; I had already poured every ounce of my being into helping Drew and Brian heal.

We returned to the porch to make a feeble attempt at finishing dinner while trying to mask our concern. I was unable to stomach even a single bite. Although Drew did not speak, he obviously knew that something was wrong.

During his time in foster care, Drew learned to be hyper-vigilant and constantly aware of his surroundings in order to maintain safety. With these learned coping mechanisms, we found hiding our troubled emotions from him to be extremely difficult. His keen sense of awareness and picked up on even the most subtle changes in voice or demeanor. Mac stomached a few more bites of his cold meal and moved inside to watch a movie as a distraction. I thought of little more than those haunting words that completely filled my heart and soul with fear.

As a former foster parent, I was always in favor of reunification of children with their birth family if it was in the best interest of the children. In this case, we had absolutely no question about the unsafe conditions of the birth family. We had a tremendous amount of evidence that deemed them unsafe and unfit to raise the boys.

Proactive was the word that the social workers from our placing agency used to describe us. Mac and I had no intentions of sitting back and letting others determine the outcome for the boys. The next morning, we immediately requested a meeting with the Department of Social Services Attorney that was assigned to our case. We were granted a time to meet the following week and made arrangements for my parents to distract the boys while we traveled four hours to the location of the meeting. The purpose of the meeting was to gather much needed information and formulate a plan.

On the day of the meeting, I felt physically ill as I entered the Department of Social Services. Drew had told us many stories about forced visits with his birth parents in that same building. I glanced around at the various rooms and wondered where those unpleasant meetings had occurred. We were escorted through an extensive maze of cubicles and finally arrived at a conference room.

We sat anxiously as we awaited the attorney who was assigned to ensure that the boys' best interest was maintained. She entered laughing and had clearly just finished a comical conversation with someone in the darkened hall. We were very thankful that she was willing to take the time to be sure we understood what was happening. Due to confidentiality constraints, she was unable to share detailed information of any sort but reiterated that we should be prepared for a long wait. As we exited the meeting, we asked if we could do anything to help this process. She simply replied, "Keep doing what you are doing. Those boys are thriving with you." The affirmation felt good, but we left with a deep need to do something more; we just did not know what.

Bah Humbug!

Beautifully decorated Christmas trees with twinkling lights were appearing in all the local stores as we dreamed of our first holiday season with Brian and Drew. Each previous Christmas, we longed to have children in our home to share all the traditional holiday experiences. We had visions of handcrafting gingerbread houses, baking cookies for Santa, and seeing excited faces as they awoke on Christmas morning to see a room filled with gifts for them to frantically enjoy. This fantasy filled my mind as I planned to make our first Christmas together unforgettable. However, as much as I was desperate to simply focus on the joy of the holiday season, the fear of the unknown loomed over me. When I glanced at their faces throughout the holiday season I wondered what thoughts consumed them. I longed to remove their emotional pain and assure them that they would remain with us forever. My newfound maternal nature came with an immense desire to protect the boys at all costs, but I was unable to shield them from emotional pain.

One day during the holidays, school had dismissed early due to an impending snow storm. We were all safely inside the house preparing to snuggle up and watch *The Grinch* when my phone rang. Since that first call warning us of a lengthy court battle, my heart froze in fear each time that my phone rang or I received an email. I knew that each communication could tell us about a new development in the court process. This time my stomach fluttered as I answered the call from Genevieve. I attempted to walk out of the room in a stealthy manner so the boys would not be alarmed. However, they knew that anytime we left the room to receive a phone call, it somehow involved their future. Even *The Grinch* did not serve as an adequate distraction when I walked into the bedroom and closed my door.

Hoping for good news, I closed my eyes while I listened intently. The social worker informed me that the birth family had hired a new attorney and were pushing to have visitation rights reinstated. A court date was set for a judge to hear all the gathered information and decide if the boys, who were now comfortable in the pre-adoptive home, would be forced to spend face-to-face time with those people who had hurt them so deeply. She instructed me to obtain letters from therapists, teachers, and other people who had close contact with Brian and Drew. We needed as much evidence as we could gather. I frantically scribbled down the court date and hung up the phone.

Running to the bathroom, I hovered over the toilet as I broke into a sweat and did everything in my power to keep from vomiting. When we welcomed the boys into our home several months earlier, we were prepared for the court process to be lengthy. However, we were assured of the fact that the case would end in adoption. Reinstating birth family visits was an indication that an attempt to reunify the children with their birth family was in process. I knew that if the boys returned to their birth family, they would experience extreme neglect and daily domestic violence. Most importantly, I wanted to protect Drew from sexual abuse by multiple family members. We were already deeply connected and attached to the boys who had been calling us Mom and Dad for months. The thought of losing them back into the system was utterly terrifying. I dropped to my bathroom floor and felt the cold tile on my face and tried to calm my out-of-control breathing. I took a deep breath and prayed for peace and guidance as I thought of the journey ahead. I prayed that God would help me to be forgiving and always put the best interest of the children in the forefront, even if that meant leaving our hearts and our home.

I knew we would need to tell the boys about the possible reinstatement of visitation and promised myself that I would not influence their opinion in this matter and vowed to respect their wishes even if it hurt me to the core. I had never heard them talk of missing anyone other than their sister, Samantha, who we were able to see on a monthly basis. I felt uncertain as to how they would respond if the opportunity to see their birth parents was presented. One thing was fairly certain: this new development would fill the days ahead with behavioral challenges, emotional meltdowns, and uncertainty. I wanted to protect the boys from these very things, but I felt powerless to accomplish that goal with this news looming over us.

Mac and I met with the boys' therapist that afternoon. We shared the details of this new development and asked advice about how to deliver the news to the boys. Armed with this advice, we directly and truthfully told the boys that their birth family wanted visitation rights to see them again. We explained that a judge would make the decision about this matter but that their opinion would be heard. We stressed that if they wanted to visit with their birth parents, we would do what we could to make it happen.

We fully expected the delivery of this news to cause emotional chaos but did not anticipate the destruction that ensued for months to follow. We had created a sense of safety, love, and permanency that the boys had never before experienced. That sense of security and safety was shattered with the delivery of one sentence. Words cannot describe the immediate level of fear, anxiety, and agitation that was exhibited by the boys at the simple mention of possible visitation. We had spent the last few months assuring them that the plan was adoption. The news of possibly seeing their birth parents overloaded their fragile minds with confusing and frightening thoughts.

Drew began to break into visible hives on his face and arms. He began shouting, "I don't ever want to see them again! Last time we had visits my birth mom didn't even take care of me when she was in the same room! I am so mad!" His voice escalated with each statement. We said nothing and simply let him shout his feelings. As I had done in the past, I moved in close proximity and put my hand on him to show support. He reached out for a very strong and powerful hug. His hugs crushed me even at a young age. He clung to me like he never wanted to let go. Nearly an hour later, his emotions finally calmed down. He reached out and expressed gratitude for the fact that he was not alone. He was able return to a brief sense of peace because he knew that we were by his side on this journey.

I suggested that he move to his desk and work on his journal. He came back downstairs with the following writing: "I do not want to see my birth parents because they have broken my heart. If I saw them I would be very upset. I have wanted to be adopted ever since I came to live here because you are great parents and I love you. If someone took me away it would break my heart into little bitty pieces." In that moment, I grieved with Drew. The grief was raw and evident. I felt indescribable pain as I watched him hurt so deeply.

As always Brian was somewhat quiet. He experienced great difficulty expressing emotion of any sort. However, this time he was motivated to share his feelings. He went directly to his journal and wrote the words: "Please tell the judge, I do not want to see our birth parents because they did not feed us. It would make me mad. I want to stay with my new Pam Mom and Mac Dad."

The responses written in both boys' journals were loud and clear; they had absolutely no desire to have contact with their birth parents.

The following days were filled with repeated oppositions to seeing their birth parents in the form of handwritten notes to the judge, letters to the social workers, conversations with therapists and massive emotional meltdowns. We had no doubt that the boys were obviously and adamantly opposed to seeing their birth parents and had an all consuming desire to be adopted.

The court date with possibility of forced visits with the birth parents had already placed emotions and fear at an all-time high. Seven days before Christmas, Genevieve came for her monthly visit. She exited her car with an armload of Christmas gifts. We assumed that the gifts were from the Department of Social Services. However, she called Mac and me aside and explained that the gifts were from the birth family. She had been ordered by the court to deliver them to the children. Knowing that the gifts were going to fuel the fire of their deep burning fear, she hesitantly handed them over with a sincere apology. I felt nauseous as I thought about the possible trauma that the delivery of these gifts would create. I swallowed heavily and reminded myself that the delivery of the gifts was court-ordered. We would have been breaking the law if we did not deliver the gifts that I knew were going to cause extreme emotional pain.

We reluctantly called the boys into the living room with as little emotion on our face as possible. After they were both comfortably seated, we explained that their birth family members had sent gifts for them. Their reaction was one of total confusion. We urged them to open the gifts. As they ripped open the gifts, I nearly bit a hole in my lip while trying to contain my emotion. I kept reminding myself that these material items meant nothing. These boys wanted and needed the gift of safety, guidance and love that every child deserves. The birth family was unwilling or unable to provide those basic gifts but were now sending material items in a feeble attempt to show love. My heart softened a bit as I realized that this may have been the only way they knew to show love.

While I felt sickened, I supported Brian as he opened the gifts one by one. He remained emotionless as he unwrapped each and every gift. When he finished opening the gifts, he moved to his stocking and unwrapped one piece of chocolate. We watched inquisitively as he then methodically gathered all of the gift items into a pile in the middle of the floor. Confused, we questioned his actions. He very calmly responded, "I don't want this stuff. Give it to the homeless people." We assured him that he could decide what to do with his gifts. He then calmly walked away to go and play with his other favorite toys. I was highly impressed by his ability to turn down material items based on the negative emotion attached to them. He was very young but had clear boundaries in his mind that he was unwilling to cross.

Drew had a very different reaction. He had always been very vocal and unable to hide his strong and heartfelt emotions. He looked at me and angrily stated, "I am confused. Why would they want to give me gifts when they didn't even take care of me?" In my best attempt at remaining positive I said, "They love you and wanted you to have these presents." His anger became more obvious as he broke out in hives and began to obsessively pick at his already raw lip. His voice elevated as he launched into an emotional tirade. "Does that mean that I am not staying here and not getting adopted?" He began repeating the phrase, "No, I'm not! No, I'm not! They are not going to put me back!" He slipped into an uncontrollable frenzy of emotion. In the past, we had learned that Mac's hugs were able to sooth and break these emotional moments of trauma. So Mac quickly responded with a firm hug and held him for 30 minutes. Held tightly in Mac's arms, his anger eventually transformed into a flood of tears. As we talked through this reaction with Drew later, we learned that, in addition to extreme fear, he was also angry at us for delivering those gifts to him. When he learned that we did not have a choice about giving him the gifts, his anger toward us was relieved.

We knew that the days ahead would undoubtedly be filled with fear, but we aimed to somehow salvage our first Christmas together. Distraction was in our favor since we were only one week away from Christmas. We were concerned that this could be our first and last Christmas together, so we attempted to share all of our Christmas traditions with them. We fought the large crowds at the mall and shopped. The boys took a great deal of time selecting gifts for each of our family members whom they had grown to love. Drew spent hours attempting to wrap the gifts he purchased. His gifts were a disastrous mess covered in mounds of tape, but they were clearly from his heart. He beamed with a sense of pride as he carefully placed the gifts under the sparkling tree in our living room.

Christmas was not complete without the traditional visit to Santa. We instructed the boys to create their Christmas wish list and be prepared to present it to Santa during our next trip to the mall. As we approached the jolly Santa imposter, the boys giggled with joy. They approached Santa together out of sheer excitement and happily climbed onto his welcoming lap. After they settled on his lap, Santa asked, "So what do you want for Christmas this year, little boys?"   Brian and Drew looked him directly in the face and simultaneously responded with one simple word. They did not ask for legos or cars; they asked for adoption! Santa looked completely perplexed by the single word uttered by the precocious boys. I felt an explanation was needed based on the baffled look displayed by the confused St. Nick. After hearing the short version of the story, Santa was moved to tears and leaned in quietly and said ,"I think you will get what you want this year." Then he glanced lovingly in our direction and offered a wink. Little did Santa know that my only wish for Christmas was the same; I wanted the gift of knowing the boys were safe and would remain with us forever.

We were all exhausted after fighting crowds and long lines at the mall so I decided to turn on some calming Christian music to soothe us on the ride home. The words that emanated from the car speaker caused each of us to become silent. The Steven Curtis Chapman song entitled, "All I Really Want For Christmas is a Family" played. The poignant words of the song told a story about a boy awaiting adoption. His only request for Christmas was a family. We carefully listened to each word of the song that sounded like it was written specifically for our family. Drew looked up at me and said,"This song is for us, isn't it?" I quickly answered, "Absolutely, it is."

Christmas morning finally arrived. The boys sounded like a herd of water buffalo as their little feet bounded down the steep steps. Mac and I had stayed up late into the previous night preparing the living room with a train set, gifts, and of course an empty plate left behind from Santa indulging in our homemade chocolate chip cookies. The morning was perfect! Brian and Drew stood in shock to take in the beautiful visual of a living room that looked like a department store. They opened gift after gift and showed such enthusiasm and gratitude for every single item including the obligatory socks and underwear. They wanted the gift process to move slowly as they savored every moment. I was deeply moved when I saw how much joy they received when giving us the gifts from them. Drew and Brian, who never had material items of their own, clearly gained more satisfaction out of giving than receiving.

We enjoyed a traditional Christmas brunch at the home of my mom and dad whom the boys lovingly referred to as Gram and Pop. Gram prepared a holiday feast including homemade biscuits and gravy, egg casserole, fruit, and special snowman shaped donuts that brought a sheepish grin to Brian's face. After time with the grandparents, we returned home to enjoy a wonderful gourmet meal together to close out the special day.

As the sun began to fade, happiness and excitement was replaced by sadness and anxiety. Drew's emotions grew out of control until he exhibited non-compliance. We asked him to go to his room for a few minutes in order to calm down. After 15 minutes passed, I became concerned and went upstairs to check on him. I entered his room to find him curled in the fetal position sobbing. He immediately hopped up, ran to me, and shouted as he said, "What if this is the only Christmas I will ever have? I have never had one like this. What if this is our only one together? I want to stay here, and I am afraid they are going to take me away!"

My heart sank as I once again watched uncertainty and fear consume this precious boy. This look of uncertainty had become very familiar. Wishing I could provide him with the assurance he needed, I kept my verbiage vague and talked about the fun times we would have together in the days ahead. Little did we know that the days ahead would be consumed by fear and uncertainty beyond our worst imagination.

As we struggled through the fear and uncertainty, I attempted to draw closer to God. However, I began to question his will and tried to understand why this journey had become so painful. I felt my faith beginning to fail. My strength was fading.

The Fear Sets In

After the holidays passed, fear, uncertainty, and constant discussions of pending court dates became the unfortunate norm in our household. Nearly every conversation, journal entry, drawing, therapy session, and family meeting revolved around the fear of leaving our home. The angst consumed the boys. As parents, we made futile attempts at disguising our worry, but both boys became very accustomed to reading our mannerisms, changes in vocal tone, and other very subtle clues. We failed at hiding the pain that hid under the surface of our encouragement for them.

As the court date approached, significant behavioral challenges continued to surface due to the boys' fear of being removed from our home. We aimed to take one day at a time in order to not become overwhelmed.   I struggled with feelings of utter helplessness because I was unable to remove their trepidation. Every aspect of life felt out of control. In those out of control moments, I often found myself with nothing left to do but surrender everything to God. In the midst of those brief moments of surrender and faith in God's plan, I found peace. However, they were short lived in spite of my best efforts.

Our entire family unit was obviously filled with stress that could not be tamed by individual effort, so we decided to tackle the issues as a team that we named Team Taylor. We talked at length about the value of relying on God and one another. We met in the living room for daily family meetings, established family goals, and prayed together for a sense of peace and acceptance of God's will. The boys responded well to that approach and requested Team Taylor hats, shirts and other items that displayed our family logo. They found strength in knowing that we were in this chaos together.

Despite our efforts to ensure emotional safety, both Brian and Drew clearly felt a constant fear of being removed from the only place they had ever felt safe and truly loved. As a parent who felt the need to protect her children, I was completely and utterly helpless. We witnessed the greatest levels of anxiety and fear when the social worker made her routine scheduled monthly visits. Since she had previously relocated them from one home to another, the boys were convinced, beyond reason, that she was coming to relocate them once again.

Nervous behaviors spiked in the days prior to scheduled visits.

Because Brian was so young he rarely spoke about his feelings but often exhibited his fear through actions instead. He chewed his fingers to the point of bleeding on a daily basis. Brian frequently locked all the doors in the house, set our alarm system at unnecessary times, and developed a refusal to go upstairs without an adult remaining in a two foot radius of him. Tugging on the front door and realizing we had been locked out became an ongoing problem. We did not want to punish Brian for locking us out of the house because we knew that his actions were based on fear. However, when he locked us out for the third time, we knew that we had to create some consequences. He was required to earn money to create extra keys. Mac and I eventually took a trip to Home Depot and made multiple copies of our key and buried them in various locations in the yard in order to avoid future lockouts.

Brian's fear became disturbingly clear as we attempted to locate him after children's church one afternoon. I walked to the room to retrieve him as always, and my heart skipped a beat when I was unable to spot his precious blue eyes in the classroom. Attempting to remain calm, I located Mac and we began searching the church building. After five minutes passed, we became panicked. We informed the church leadership and they began a methodical search of the church grounds. In that moment, I feared I had lost Brian forever. With tears in my eyes and total terror in my heart, I entered the preschool classroom hoping that he had gone in to play with some of the toys that he had seen earlier in the day. I scanned the room but saw nothing. The silence was deafening.

All of my worst fears began to surface until I glanced down at a small table that was covered in a gingham cloth. I saw a small untied shoe sticking out of the side. I recognized it as Brian's. I lifted the cloth while clinging to my one last hope and breathed a giant sigh of relief when I saw him curled in a small, tight ball. As I reached for him he immediately shushed me, whispering, "Shhh, I am hiding." When asked why he was hiding, he responded with a frightened whisper, "I am afraid they are going to take me away from you." With uncontrollable emotion I scooped him up into my arms, grasped him tight and simply said, "I've got you, and I am never letting go." He wrapped his arms around my neck and clearly felt a sense of relief that I was not angry about his actions. He clung onto my neck like never before as we exited the room and told the others he had been found.

While both boys were completely debilitated by worry and fear, Drew was a lot more vocal about his fears. He spoke of them daily, but we were only able to soothe him for very brief periods of time. Drew walked around with a hood pulled over his head. His lips bled constantly because he had nervously picked until no skin remained. We realized that his anxiety was not going to dissipate until they were with us permanently. Almost every night at bedtime, he broke out in hives, followed by an overabundance of sweat, rapid breathing, and an obvious sense of terror. I spent those sleepless nights rocking Drew in a large leather rocking chair in our living room. The repetitive motion and physical contact calmed him from what were obvious panic attacks. My arms and legs went numb as I rocked him for hours at a time and softly whispered into his ear that he was safe and loved. I savored these treasured moments when Drew proved to me that I had become a force strong enough to offer a brief sense of security and safety for him. Drew also obviously treasured these moments. He seemed to deeply crave these actions by a loving mother that he missed as an infant. As he fell asleep in my exhausted arms, he repeatedly whispered phrases about wanting a normal life and thanked me for helping him. Those moments created an impenetrable bond between us. Any moment of peace I was able to deliver in the midst of this pain was a gift for both of us.

The day of the court proceeding finally arrived. While were not present at the court, we anxiously awaited news from the social worker. We had prepared well for this event. We had submitted letters from therapists, teachers, and counselors. The boys had also written letters, stating their desire to cut all contact from their birth parents.

Approximately one hour after the court was scheduled to be completed, our phone rang. The initial news offered a sense of relief. They told us that the birth family was not granted visitation with the boys. However, in the sentence that followed, we were informed that we had a significant battle ahead. Lilith was determined to fight. As the maternal birth grandmother, she had a longstanding history with the Department of Social Services. She had a documented history of delusional behavior. In court, she had accused the judge of taking bribes, claimed that God had spoken to her directly, and had been asked to leave the courtroom on several occasions for her aggressive actions toward social workers and court employees. She hired a private attorney who was going to fight the decision of the Department of Social Services and the Guardian Ad Litem in terminating parental rights. This was a devastating blow. Brian and Drew desperately needed permanency; helping them function in the state of uncertainty that had consumed them for the past eight months was an overwhelming prospect.

Most of the time, I am not easily angered. However, I felt enraged as I hung up the phone. The birth family had been given five years to meet the minimal requirements in taking care of these two boys. Brian and Drew finally had the opportunity to have a permanent family who wanted to meet their needs. However, the birth family decided to fight as soon as they learned that the courts were attempting to terminate their parental rights.

As pre-adoptive parents, our rights were very limited. However, I spent many hours researching our options on the internet. I soon discovered that we had the right to hire a private attorney to represent us in this case. Mac and I were in agreement that we had to do everything within our grasp to fight for these boys. We had seen so much pain in their eyes. We were ready to fight for them.

Darth Vader

We were determined to locate the best attorney possible to represent us as we moved forward. I spent so much time doing research on the computer that pain from carpal tunnel syndrome began to pierce my wrists on a daily basis. A sense of strength and empowerment came with the realization that we had the ability to do something to help fight for the boys. Eight months of helplessness had taken its toll, and we needed to feel that our thoughts and opinions mattered in some way. The only way to achieve that goal was to hire a private attorney.

Each and every time we asked which attorney was the most feared in the county where the court would convene we received the same response: Ann Cunningham.

Feeling confident in our decision, we loaded the car with our binders of data, journal writings, and other documentation and set out on the four-hour ride to her office and hoped that she would take our case. Her services we highly sought after, and we feared that something would stop her from leading our charge.

After a few hours in the car we caught a glimpse of some impressive scenery in the quaint, little waterfront town and felt a sense of hope for the first time in months. We located a parking spot under a large willow tree and entered the law office in a historic building within walking distance to the courthouse. A large fish tank in the lobby of the law office caught my attention. My nervous excitement was calmed by watching the clown fish swim repetitively back and forth between the underwater plastic statues and fake coral. The office was bustling with activity and we could find no available seats. I paced back and forth and occasionally glanced across the street at the courthouse where our future would be determined.

We finally heard our names called and followed the paralegal into a beautiful conference room that was decorated with a large, ornate conference table and some antique armchairs with burgundy velvet seats. We waited nervously for the attorney to arrive.

Finally, we heard high heels clicking against the aged, wooden floor. The sound of clicking heels grew louder until Ann Cunningham entered the room with a confidence like none I had ever seen. She was dressed in a black, classy business suit with black heels. Her hair was pulled away from her face that had a very stern look. I felt immediately intimidated and thankful that she was going to be on our side. She softened the mood by smiling and sarcastically stating, "So, what can I bring to this party?" We laughed and began to share details about the case as she attentively took notes. Her demeanor softened further as she learned that we required representation to ensure that the best interest of two boys in foster care was being met. She revealed that she had been adopted as a teen and held this issue close to her heart. We mutually agreed that permanency was in the best interest of the children and she would do everything in her power to ensure that this case moved quickly. She stepped out for a brief moment to make a few phone calls and returned to tell us that she would take our case. We were truly relieved and felt a sense of security in knowing that this attorney, who had been described as a pitbull in the courtroom, was going to fight on behalf of the best interest of Brian and Drew.

My heart sank as she delivered the payment schedule. I knew attorneys were expensive, but had no idea where we would obtain the initial retainer. Mac and I decided before attending the meeting that we would commit no matter the cost. We stepped out on faith and accepted the payment schedule in order to secure her legal services, knowing that we needed to locate $8000 to get the process started. We knew that we had the support of family and friends who would help us meet this need. More importantly, we trusted God to provide if this was His plan. Adoption through the foster care system was supposed to be free, but we felt the need to utilize all possible resources on behalf of these children. As we returned to our car with a sense of empowerment, Mac looked at me and uttered in a very calm voice, "I think we just hired the female version of Darth Vader."

Never Say Never!

When starting the adoption process, we had an extensive list of stipulations. This list included specific scenarios, situations, and behaviors that we were not willing to accept under any circumstance. We stated to our placing agency that we were unwilling to accept a child over the age of five. Due to my extensive background in child development, I was very aware of the importance of the early years. We also stated that we would never accept a sibling group. We had our minds set on one child. In addition, we were adamantly opposed to a legal risk placement, meaning that the child was not legally free for adoption. Ignorantly, we were also certain we would never accept a child who had been sexually abused since we did not have much background or training in this area. Lastly, we very firmly stated that we would never be willing to have face-to-face contact with the birth parents.

That final stipulation pointed to one of my greatest fears in the midst of this fight - meeting the birth parents. So much emotion was tied into the thought of standing face-to-face with the adults who were given the gift of two beautiful boys but were unable or unwilling to provide for their very basic needs. While I clearly had no control over this possibility, I vowed that I would avoid this contact if at all possible.

We had created the list of stipulations to protect ourselves and give us what we thought was the best outcome. Instead, God amazingly pulled us out of our comfort zone and shattered our boxed plan the second we met Drew and Brian.

After we hired the private attorney, the Department of Social Services began inviting us to planning meetings. In addition, our attorney provided us with information about the case details. She also kept us up to date on court proceedings. At that point, I had been forced to let go of any sense of control and simply trust God one day at a time as I hung on for dear life.

We quickly realized the value in hiring a private attorney. She began to dig into the details of this case. Soon after she took our case, she received word that the birth father had contacted his attorney because he was planning to leave his wife and was considering a voluntary relinquishment of his parental rights. The attorneys felt that if we met him in person, he would be more likely to make this consideration a definite decision.

However, the maternal side of the family was unaware of the birth father's plans. They were expected to become angry if they discovered his plan. We became hopeful since a voluntary relinquishment was the ideal situation for all involved. If he was willing to sign his parental rights away, we could potentially avoid the impending court battle, the boys would have the permanency they craved, and we could someday report to them that their birth father had put their needs ahead of his own. Having vowed to do everything possible to achieve permanency for the boys, we tossed our fears of meeting him in person aside and stepped out on faith one more time as we solidified plans to meet face to face with the birth father.

Mac and I were both filled with anxiety as we traveled the familiar road back to the place where the boys were born. We were cautiously optimistic that we might be able to make some positive ground by showing their birth father that they were thriving in our care. Mac and I were both silent during the road trip. I glanced out the window and imagined what their birth father looked like. I wondered how much Brian and Drew looked like those who gave birth to them. While it was very difficult for me to fathom the thought of people causing such harm to their children, I felt an underlying sense of compassion for this man whom I had never met. As we neared the attorney's office, I prayed that God would remove any anger from my heart and that the words that flowed from my mouth would be those of kindness and compassion. I also prayed that the birth father would open his heart and mind to see how much we loved the boys who had been in our home for nearly nine months.

We pulled our car down the bumpy cobblestone street in the historic area of town and attempted to parallel park on the very narrow road. Mac grasped my hand as we entered the office of the attorney that had been appointed to the the birth father, Cameron. The attorney promptly greeted us and escorted us to a very small conference room and left us at the entrance. Without warning, the door creaked open. My hopes of a voluntary relinquishment were immediately dashed when I saw a female sitting directly next to whom I assumed was Cameron. We drove four hours in anticipation of a private meeting with the birth father, but he was not alone. I felt the adrenaline pierce my veins as every ounce of me wanted to turn and run, but that was not a viable option. We were face-to-face with the man and woman who had given birth to Drew and Brian.

I felt like the walls were closing in on me as I attempted to slow my breathing. I reminded myself that this was for Drew and Brian, and I pushed my own needs aside. To say that the greeting was awkward does not adequately describe that moment. Mac and I cordially shook their hands and introduced ourselves. My heart was pounding so hard that I felt sure they could see my shirt moving up and down rhythmically with each beat. Cameron was a very quiet and meek man who was clearly uncomfortable. He made very minimal eye contact and spent a great deal of time staring at the floor. Blair, the birth mother, sat directly across from me. My immediate impression was that she looked as if she was not present in the room. I cannot find the words to adequately describe the empty and hollow look on her face. I assumed that tears would flow as she met the people who were caring for her children. Instead, she showed no tears. Actually, she showed no emotion at all. Her flat and monotone voice matched her emotionless demeanor.

In our typical overachieving fashion, Mac and I had prepared a PowerPoint presentation to show Cameron pictures and data about the boys' progress. Since we had prepared to talk about a voluntary relinquishment, we included many slides about how the boys had become deeply attached to Mac and me and how they had been unwavering in their expression of a desire to remain with our family forever. Feelings of sadness washed over me as I closely watched their reactions. Once again, I expected them to weep as they viewed picture after picture of the boys whom they had not seen for many months.

Cameron was clearly interested in their progress and asked questions about their activities, school, church, and other parts of daily life. However, Blair remained completely stoic as picture after picture showed how happy her children were without her. As the conversation continued, I considered the possibility that she was employing a coping response of some sort and would eventually burst into an uncontrollable expression of love and desire for her children. The response never came. No response at all ever surfaced. I was truly heartbroken at her lack of emotion. I desperately wanted to hear her say that she loved and missed her children. I needed to believe that she loved them deeply and simply could not care for them. At times I was tempted to tell her the words she needed to say. She continued to stare blankly as we continued to talk.

As the conversation progressed, we began to realize that a discussion about relinquishment of parental rights would not occur at this meeting. Despite the fact that their birth mother had been told that the court was moving toward a termination of parental rights to move toward adoption, she unemotionally referred to getting her children back in the near future. She was clearly out of touch with reality and was absolutely certain that we were raising her children on a very temporary basis. Mac and I were very kind and supportive and explained that we would always respect them as the boys' birth parents. We were hopeful that they could see how much we loved Brian and Drew. We wanted to send the clear message that we were in no way trying to take their children from them, but would love them and care for them if they were unable.

Feelings of utter disappointment and confusion overwhelmed us as we left the conference room. We stopped to question Cameron's attorney as we exited and demanded answers regarding Blair's presence at the meeting. He simply stated that he did not know she was coming and that he was sorry for the inconvenience. The meeting had been useless, and I felt sickened as I walked back to our car. We were back to square one and knew we had a difficult battle ahead.

The car ride home was very somber. I simply wanted to rush home and give the boys hugs in an attempt to take the hurt away. The small glimpse that I had of their birth mother was haunting. I was certain that she loved the children in some way but was completely unable to communicate that love. Meeting the people who gave birth to the boys had been very eye opening in many ways. Although our encounter with them was brief, the complete lack of emotion, demonstration of ideas that were out of touch with reality, and total lack of understanding regarding the needs of the boys made it blatantly obvious that Cameron and Blair were completely unable to parent the boys.

In the days following our encounter, I was motivated to wake up every morning and show the boys that they were loved beyond measure and absolutely precious to us. I had a deep desire to make up for what they had missed for so many years: the loving affection of a mother.

Name Change

Change was what the boys had desired from an early age. They wished for nothing more than to escape their life of trauma. After 4 years of uncertainty and constant moves, they had landed in the arms of our family who equipped them with feelings of safety and love. As time progressed, they confirmed their desire for permanency more and more.

Brian bounded down the steps at least twice a week asking to watch Adoption Stories on television. This was a show about various types of adoption. Every episode had a storybook ending that involved a completed adoption followed by a celebration. One particular morning, we watched an episode about a child who was adopted at the age of thirteen. He had spent six years in foster care before finding his forever family.

This particular episode depicted Drew and Brian's fantasy of a finalized adoption in the courtroom. The teen in the episode legally changed both his first and last name after his adoption was complete to serve as a fresh start. The name change enabled him to leave his difficult past behind. Drew was very attentive to this episode and asked us to record it only a few minutes after the show began. I obliged and recorded the episode.

After the show was over, I moved to the kitchen and began cleaning. I watched from a distance as both boys played the episode again and again. This particular episode obviously touched them on a deep level. After they had watched it the fourth time in a row, I approached and initiated a conversation about it. Drew immediately looked up and, without hesitation, said, "I want to change my name." I carefully explained that, if and when the adoption was completed, their last name would change to Taylor. Drew chimed in again and said, "No, I want to change my whole name, every bit of it."   Brian then agreed and said he desired to do the same. My suggestion was to slow down and take some significant time to think about this life-changing decision.

We had a scheduled therapy appointment the next week, so I insisted that the possible name change be the topic of conversation. I understood that they had a desire to have a fresh start, but I was concerned that this was a decision that they would regret later in life. Both boys were insistent and talked about little else for days. I remained neutral and simply listened as they tried out different names for one another.

I emailed the therapist before our appointment and expressed my concerns about them making a hasty decision about name changes. She was prepared for the conversation in our session five days later. They each had individual sessions and went in one at a time. Toward the end of our session, she called Mac and me in for an important conversation. She very confidently stated that each of the boys had thought through the ramifications of the name change, and she felt that they were ready to make this change. When they left the room, I reminded her that we were not even certain that the adoption was going to occur. She replied, "They need this." She reminded us that nothing would change legally unless we adopted them, but they needed to feel the sense of empowerment and change that came along with a decision such as this. Her explanation made sense, so we agreed to let them select new names. They had changed in many ways since arriving, and this would solidify those changes and allow them to leave the past behind.

I found myself in the local bookstore, selecting a book of names for the boys to use as a resource. The thick book, with an infant plastered on the front cover had pages and pages of names with their corresponding meanings.

Brian selected his name rather quickly. He liked the name Michael because it meant "Of God". However, Drew spent hours flipping through the book while he sat alone at the table on our screened in porch. After much consideration, he narrowed it down to four possibilities before presenting his findings. When he read the definitions, his new name became Trent. Trent was a perfect fit. The definition in the book defined the name as "strength." After disclosing so much horrific abuse, he had begun to feel strong.

We all agreed to call the boys Michael and Trent from that point forward. We all had hope that we would be legally changing the names in a few short months. Until that time, we chose to call them the new names they selected as a symbolic expression of change.

Court Draws Near

Since childhood, I have loved the thrill of the unknowns in a roller coaster ride: the seat clicking as it moves slowly up the steep track, the sheer terror as it travels up and down at high rates of speed, the knots in the stomach from the sharp twists and turns. This journey to adoption was like a roller coaster without the happy excitement. From day one, we had experienced so many ups and downs, twists and turns, moments of fear, and the necessity to strap in and prepare for a crazy ride. Our emotions had been in turmoil for ten months. One minute we heard everything was fine and that the boys would remain with us forever, and the next we heard that they would remain in foster care to give the birth family additional time to prove that they could parent. I learned to be prepared for twists and turns and to simply cling to God in every moment. I felt certain that God was going to use this experience to grow each of us in some manner, despite the outcome. I was so deeply attached and in love with Trent and Mike that the thought of losing

145

them was enough to destroy me. I lived every day with an upset stomach, dull headache and other symptoms associated with stress and anxiety. I was forced to watch them struggle daily as they pushed through the anxiety and uncertainty.

My inability to reduce their stress and anxiety took me to places of deep sadness. I was their mom in my heart, and a mother's role is to protect her children from pain. No matter how many words of comfort I delivered, I was unable to say the words they longed to hear: words saying that they were never leaving.

I often equated our journey with that of someone parenting a child with a significant illness. When a child is chronically ill, a parent cannot remove the pain. Consumed by helplessness, all they can do is remain by a child's side and offer support as they experience the pain and suffering. At least when faced with a physical illness, medications and treatments can often ease the suffering. Although my children were not battling a physical illness, they were faced with horrific memories on a daily basis that attacked their emotional well being and ability to function. Not a day went by when I did not strive to minimize their emotional pain, but I could find little to do to ease it. I would have given anything to trade places with them and suffer in their place. I had to remind myself daily that God was in control.

As court approached, our days were filled with phone conferences, lengthy road trips to meet with the attorney, therapy sessions, Team Taylor family meetings, and time with friends and family who had stepped up to form an army of support. We also spent much time in prayer during these dark days of uncertainty.

During this time, the song, "Waiting" played daily on the local Christian radio stations. This became my personal theme song, and I sang along to the words that resonated with me. The song spoke of waiting on the Lord and the pain that often accompanies lengthy waits. It spoke of moving ahead with boldness and confidence to serve the Lord despite circumstances. My mind was a daily battlefield as I struggled to serve God each day in the midst of great pain. I cried every time I heard the song that so adequately described my life.

While I was brushing my hair one morning before church, the familiar song began to play. In that moment, I was so utterly emotionally exhausted from the never-ending fear of losing my boys that I simply dropped to the floor in a flood of tears. My body, mind, and spirit were all broken in that moment. I heard Trent approaching and wanted to pull myself up to my feet and quickly wipe away my tears to hide the pain, but he entered the room before I mustered the strength. He knew the reason for my tears and quickly approached me falling to the floor by my side. He took me into his sweet, pre-adolescent arms and held me while I cried tears of deep pain and sorrow. I clearly confused him because my crying escalated when he embraced me. I mumbled through my tears enough to get the message across that I was crying because I loved them so much. He wrapped his arms around me and comforted me as I had comforted him so many times in the past. He said, "Mom, I love you, and you need to remember that God has a plan for us." I was truly humbled and broken in that moment by his child-like faith and confidence. He was absolutely correct, and I felt a peace come over me as I heard his poignant words. We remained on the floor in a loving hug for what seemed like an eternity. My love for Trent and Mike had grown far deeper than I ever imagined possible. I had always heard that a mother's love for her children in indescribable. I knew in that moment exactly what those words meant.

Rolling on the River

As court approached, negative behaviors escalated, panic attacks increased, and anger toward those who had hurt Trent and Mike in the past was a consistent theme.

Since anger was prevalent, we developed activities to help alleviate these deep-seeded emotions. A punching bag was placed in Trent's room, physical exercise was encouraged, and journaling about thoughts and feelings was a daily requirement. We also frequently visited a local river and walking trail to get some much needed fresh air and clear our heads. The water that rippled over the large rocks was a familiar soothing sound for each of us. We visited the therapeutic river almost weekly and parked ourselves on the large rocks to watch the water flow. We all found a deep sense of peace when sitting there as a family.

After school one cool spring afternoon, Trent firmly stated, "I need to go to the river." He was learning to manage his anger and knew when it was building, so his request to visit the river was granted. When we arrived at our destination, we settled into our usual spot and got comfortable. Trent was agitated and more active than usual. In an attempt to redirect him, I encouraged him to see if he could skip rocks by throwing them into the flowing water.

As he gathered pebbles of various sizes the sides of his cheeks turned cherry red. He began throwing the stones with all his might and seemed to enjoy seeing them pound into the water with power. He looked our direction and shouted, "I am going to throw rocks in the water because I am mad." He then stated, "I am going to pretend the water is my birth parents." During the last few months, Mac and I had learned to be supportive by allowing Trent to process his pain as he chose to process it as long as he was safe and the methods were appropriate. This activity met the criteria, so we allowed it to continue as we watched from a distance in amazement as this emotionally driven nine-year-old boy processed some of his deepest pain. He grabbed up one rock at a time and with each throw he shouted a different offense at the top of his lungs, "This one is for not taking care of us! This one is for not feeding us! This one is for not keeping us safe!" His anger was building with each throw. He continued on, "This one is for not bathing us! This one is for not tucking us in at night! This one is for not reading to us! This one is for letting people do bad things to us!" He continued on and on and tears began to flow down his cheeks as he launched each painful memory into the rapids to be washed away. He ran out of rocks and grabbed a handful of twigs that he angrily tossed into the river.

Trent then approached Mac and grabbed a wooden boat that they had made together, looked us directly in the face and said, "This boat is my birth parents." Then he placed it on the ground, stomped on it with all of his might, threw rocks at it, and tossed it into the water yelling, "You were horrible parents!" As he watched the boat float away, he said, "Goodbye, get out of here!"

As Mike watched Trent, he realized the therapeutic benefit of the activity and eventually joined him. I wiped my tears as I watched their pain symbolically float down the rapids, wishing that I had a way to make their pain float away like the boat had floated away.

Finally, Trent, tired and covered with sweat, climbed into my lap and said, "I love you both so much. Why weren't you there when we were little?" Knowing that the sentence was illogical, he simply moved on by saying, "I just can't wait anymore; I just can't!"

Trent then stood on the edge of the large rock and announced, "Now I am going to throw rocks for the good things you have done for me." We remained completely silent while we watched him gently skip rocks and utter a positive praise with each toss, "This is for keeping me safe. This is for loving me. This is for teaching me math. This is for spending time with me." As the comments continued, we realized that this was his way of thanking us for the unconditional love we had offered to him. My heart ached as I grasped onto my family and wished for nothing more than to know that I would never have to let go.

Wishful Thinking

Not a day passed when we did not find Trent and Mike counting down the days on the calendar that hung on our refrigerator. Each crossed-off day moved us one day closer to the court date. We made frequent attempts to shield them from any information that we thought would cause them anxiety, but they were fixated on the upcoming events, making the task nearly impossible.

An overwhelming desire for adoption was the theme in almost every activity that took place in our house. Pretend adoptions happened very frequently with stuffed animals, nutcrackers, GI Joe action figures and our pets. Trent pretended to be the judge who confirmed the adoption. Homemade adoption decrees were awarded to all of the pretend adoptees.

Mike had many stuffed animals, but he had a favorite stuffed guinea pig that my mother gave him shortly after he arrived. He resisted emotional conversations with adults, but we often overheard him having very detailed, emotion-filled conversations with his stuffed guinea pig who had been by his side in bed each and every night since his arrival.

Mac and I tucked both boys into bed every single night with conversation, a story or two, prayer, and hugs. One night on our way up the stairs to tuck Mike into bed, we overheard him conversing with his guinea pig, "You don't have to be afraid anymore. Tomorrow you will be getting adopted, and no one can come and take you away. You won't have to worry about getting hurt anymore." Mac and I embraced each other as we listened to these heart-felt wishes for a dream to come true.

Trent and Mike began telling everyone they knew about their desire to be adopted. They seemed to be trying to speak their adoption into becoming a reality. However, their fear also escalated each day as they checked the calendar and the court date loomed over them.

We lived within walking distance to a wonderful park equipped with an extensive piece of climbing equipment, swings, and a large open area to run and play. I frequently sat on the bench and soaked up the sun while the boys ran around the playground. During these times of observation, I saw their "fight or flight" response as they rapidly raced around with a fake smile plastered to their faces.

On many occasions, they approached children to play and were sharing their life story with them within a matter of moments. I heard both boys often say, "We are going to get adopted. We hope so anyway. The judge is going to say, "Yes!" I often shook my head and smiled as I watched children respond with utter confusion at the unfamiliar statements. Often after an awkward pause, the children simply resumed playing. These conversations on the playground reminded me that their desire to be adopted was consuming their thoughts. I did not know how much longer they could tolerate the waiting. The mental, emotional, and physical effects were exhausting. I wanted this period of uncertainty to end.

Secret Meetings

Time slowly ticked away, and we were within a month of the big Termination of Parental Rights hearing that would determine the future for Trent and Mike. Attorneys for all parties had been preparing for the battle through research, meetings, and phone conversations. We eagerly anticipated each update from our attorney and prepared for the roller coaster ride to resume each time the phone rang.

One afternoon while I was at work, I received an unexpected phone call from the paralegal who asked if we would be willing to share our e-mail address with the birth father who was apparently reconsidering a voluntary relinquishment of his rights. We had gone down this road before and were bitterly disappointed. We cautiously agreed to create a new email account specifically to communicate with him. After the new email address was established, we checked the account every day. Again we were disappointed when nothing appeared. Updates from our attorney continued and we received unofficial word that Cameron was planning to leave his wife and move to another state. We were also informed that he was still considering relinquishment. However, he was fearful of the maternal side of the family who would likely attempt to harm him both physically and emotionally if he voluntarily signed his rights away. The dramatic scenario was developing major complications as the court date approached.

One evening as I clicked on the email account, I saw a bold message in the inbox from the birth father's attorney. The message requested a phone number. Mac did not hesitate in sending his phone number to be shared with the birth father.

When Mac's phone rang the next day while at the park, an unknown number appeared. Before answering the call, Mac walked far enough away so that the boys would not hear his conversation. The person on the other end of the line was a very timid and quiet Cameron. Offering a lot of kindness and support, Mac spoke with him for a long time, updating him about the boys. With no mention of relinquishment, Mac requested a time to meet with him in person so we could talk further.

Cameron agreed and selected a date and a time. However, Cameron seemed unwilling to commit to a specific meeting place. Instead, he requested that we call him when we arrived in town on the date of the meeting. The request seemed odd, but we complied.

A week passed and we attempted to keep the pending meeting a secret from Trent and Mike. Anxiety would have become uncontrollable if they had an indication that we were communicating with their birth parents in any way.

The lengthy car ride had become all too familiar. Each time we had taken this trip in the past, feelings of discomfort and anxiety had been overwhelming. We prayed multiple times on the way to meet with Cameron. We prayed that his heart was softened and he would have the courage to do what was in the best interest of his children that he had been unable to care for. I began to sweat as I noticed familiar landmarks and knew that we were getting close.

Finally, we reached the town and pulled into a parking space. Mac reached for his phone, called Cameron, and told him we had arrived and were sitting in the parking lot of a local shopping center. We were in a very public location and assumed that it would be a perfect spot to meet. Cameron quietly agreed to meet us in the parking lot in fifteen minutes.

When he pulled into the parking spot next to our car, his face was filled with fear and he glared in all directions and appeared to be ensuring that he had not been followed. His fear began to feed my fear. While I had expected some tension because he had not shared his intentions of possible relinquishment with the maternal side of the family, I did not expect to see complete and utter terror on his face.

Cameron quickly approached our driver's side car window. He did not give a greeting, but quickly asked if we could relocate to a place that was not so public. He expressed concern about Lilith, the maternal grandmother, and his brother-in-law, both working in the area. He was clearly fearful of being spotted speaking to us. He provided us with an address for a location that was twenty minutes away and asked us to meet him there. While we were in shock, we agreed. He returned to his car and quickly drove away.

We travelled a long straight road into a small rural town. As we drove, we saw few buildings and stores other than an occasional gas station with old fashioned pumps. Traveling to an unknown destination was frightening. We were trusting this man, who we had only met once, to lead us to a safe location.

My fear increased as we approached the address he had provided. As usual, Mac appeared calm and relaxed. While his ability to remain calm in stressful times often infuriated me, his calming nature was exactly what I needed to survive that moment.

The address took us to an outdated Exxon gas station on a gravel lot. With two old-fashioned pumps, the gas station looked like it was from the 1950's. At first, we did not see Cameron's vehicle and wondered if he had sent us on a road to nowhere. As Mac drove around behind the gas station, we spotted Cameron's vehicle in the far corner. He had clearly pulled as far off the road as possible. He was parked between two dumpsters behind the building and very clearly did not want to be seen. We pulled up next to his vehicle and asked him if we were able to talk at this location. He scanned the area in all directions and said, "Yes, this will work."

Cameron opened his car door to get into our car. As he walked toward us, I smelled the stale scent of cigarettes. The boys had shared how the smell of cigarettes reminded them of bad memories. As the scent arrested my senses, I understood why that was so bothersome to them.

Cameron hesitantly climbed into our back seat, locked the car doors, and slouched down as low as possible. He was clearly terrified, so we decided to simply ask him the reason for his fear. He shared that he was very fearful of his mother-in-law and a few of Blair's other relatives. He explained that they would be very angry at him for speaking with us and that he was fearful of actions they might take.

We thanked Cameron for putting his children ahead of his fear and proceeded to update him. We showed him pictures, told him stories, and assured him that we would give the boys the best life possible if they remained with us. He was very respectful and soft spoken. I felt empathetic as he appeared to be remorseful for his inability to care for his children. He thanked us for taking care of them and admitted that he was unable to properly care for them. Forgiveness flooded over me as I heard him take ownership for the damage that had been inflicted on his children. Although we did not directly discuss a voluntary relinquishment, we felt that the groundwork had been laid and a sense of trust had been established.

Cameron provided us with his cell phone number so we could contact him as needed. In a blink, our clandestine meeting in the back of a gas station in a small rural town came to a close as he rapidly re-entered his vehicle and pulled away with a look of sheer terror on his face. Mac and I remained in our car for a moment just to process the very strange moment that seemed like a scene out of a lifetime movie. If this meeting was any indication, the court battle ahead was going to be an adventure.

We anxiously awaited any word that our meeting had enough impact to encourage Cameron to consider putting the needs of his boys ahead of his own by offering a relinquishment.

One week later, an excited voice was on the other end of the phone when I picked up and heard the words, "Cameron voluntarily relinquished his rights." Our attorney called and delivered the news with a sense of pride and accomplishment. Cameron had voluntarily given up his parental rights without the consent of Blair. Without using her typical legal jargon, the attorney explained that Cameron had seven calendar days to change his mind. At the end of the seven day period, his rights would be forever terminated and we would only need to battle the maternal birth family in court.

The seven day wait was utter torture. The lawyers warned us that if Blair or any of the maternal birth family members found out about the father's decision, fear would force him to pull out of the relinquishment. We prayed that he would remain strong through this period and sent him e-mails and texts to encourage him and reassure him that he had made the right decision for his children.

I opened my eyes with a sense of peace and happiness on day seven. We breathed a huge sigh of relief as we confirmed with our attorney that the relinquishment was final. While this served as a temporary relief, we were all aware of the menacing court battle ahead.

Pack Your Bags

We prepared ourselves for the impending court battle to face the maternal side of the family who had a significant and documented history of mental illness, emotional instability and aggressive actions toward social workers, court employees, and others.

Only seven days remained before we were set to attend the Termination of Parental Rights hearing that we had anxiously anticipated for nearly a year. We were told to prepare for the court hearing to last anywhere from two to four days.

The hearing was scheduled for two phases that would need to be completed before the boys were legally free for adoption. The first phase was called Termination of Parental Rights. This phase would determine whether the birth mother would lose her legal rights to the children or be granted additional time in order to reunify the family. If her rights were terminated, the hearing would move on to phase two which was called "Best Interest". During the best interest phase, the judge had the job of determining if it was in the best interest to assign an adoptive placement by examining potential adoptive families. Based on past history, the average length of time for one of these hearings was typically three to four hours. Our case had become so complicated and involved that it was expected to last a number of days.

We rallied our support and put a plan in place. Rather than travel the four-hour trip each day, we arranged to stay in a beautiful beach house located twenty minutes away from the courthouse. This arrangement would allow Trent and Mike to be distracted by friends, fun, and the beach while we attended court. The plan was for us to join them in the evenings to spend some much needed family time to decompress.

As time approached, the fear of loss fueled our deep desire to spend every possible minute with the two boys who were the most emotionally vulnerable than we had ever seen them.

As I packed our clothing, toiletries and other items needed for the week ahead, I had moments of utter disbelief. In seven days, one judge was going to determine the rest of our lives as a family. I prayed that he would hear the truth from the individuals scheduled to testify on behalf of Trent and Mike. Multiple therapists, social workers, guardians ad litem, and various other experts were scheduled to testify in favor of terminating the parental rights of Blair who had been unwilling to meet very basic requirements for over five years in order to keep her children.

As foster parents, we had no legal rights to the boys and would not be permitted to testify. However, my background in child development and extensive background in behavior management qualified me as an official behavioral expert, so I was scheduled to testify specifically regarding behavioral changes and other related topics. For nearly a year, I had yearned to have a voice and was now counting down the moments until I could take the stand to speak to the judge on behalf of my boys. Not knowing when I would be called to testify, I needed to be prepared from the minute we entered the courtroom. I was mentally prepared to speak the truth, but did not feel confident about my emotional readiness. While I was motivated to speak on their behalf, I struggled with a fear that I would be unable to contain my emotions that had been building over the past year.

My anger toward Cameron had diminished since he took ownership of his mistakes. However, Blair and her mother, Lilith, maintained the stance that they had done nothing wrong and had given the children a wonderful childhood. My negative feelings toward the maternal side of the family had grown exponentially over time as I heard stories of using religion inappropriately, threats of violence to anyone who spoke in a manner that may expose the extensive history of abuse and cult-like behavior, the accusation that the judge had taken bribes from the Department of Social Services, and even more accusations of D.S.S. being influenced by the devil. Blair's loss of touch with reality was going to cost us nearly $30,000 in attorney fees and significant emotional stress. It had also left Mike and Trent in a state of complete and total turmoil their entire lives.

As a strong Christian, I truly struggled with my inability to move beyond my anger and work toward a place of forgiveness. While I still worked toward forgiveness, I found freedom after having conversations with multiple pastors who reminded me that righteous anger was not a sin, especially when protecting children. I just needed to be careful in how I channeled those feelings. I prayed that I would be able to keep my emotions under control once I was in the courtroom and on the witness stand.

Close family and friends gathered at our pastor's house the night before we left for court. We spent significant time on our knees in prayer as a group. Both Mike and Trent uttered the same prayer that we heard hundreds of times over the past few months. They repeatedly uttered their desperate plea to remain with our family forever. In addition to a group prayer, a family friend arranged for hourly prayer each day while we were in court. It provided a sense of calm in the storm to know that prayer warriors were going to be on their knees praying for a positive outcome for our family throughout our battle. We drove home in silence as we all stared out the windows, each facing our own fears about the days ahead.

As we pulled into the driveway of our home, I couldn't help but wonder if this was our last night together. The boys requested to sleep on the floor on either side of our bed that night. We were more than happy to oblige so that we could feel the closeness that we feared would soon be gone. Several times during the night Trent reached up from the floor and grasped my hand for comfort. My eyes were burning from the salty tears that were flowing non-stop as I tried to sleep in preparation for the most important day of our lives. I eventually drifted off to sleep.

I startled as the alarm sounded at 5:00 a.m. I desperately wanted to close my eyes and believe the planned trip before us was all a nightmare. Instead, reality took over the morning, and we quickly got dressed and ready for the all too familiar drive to the town of the boys' birth and early childhood, hoping this was the final drive to that place in this fight for justice. Joining us for the trip to provide moral support were my mom and our best friends at the time, Brent and Kathy Powers. My father remained at home in order to care for the pets at our houses. The boys greeted my mom with a loving embrace and were pleased that she was coming along; she had always provided them with a nurturing sense of security and comfort.

The ride seemed like an eternity as we passed all the familiar landmarks and buildings. I glanced down the side streets that we passed and wondered which of these roads held their secrets and past trauma.

This was the first time the boys had travelled back into the area since coming to join our family. Hives broke out, heart rates increased, and both boys sought extreme comfort as we traveled through the town that was filled with terrorizing memories. Trent pointed out familiar landmarks and businesses. He was very visibly shaken as we traveled down this very painful memory lane. Fortunately, we passed through quickly and headed to the beach house in order to prepare them for the day.

Both boys attempted to remain strong as we kissed each of them on their heads, offered soothing hugs, and told them how much we loved them. They made a brave attempt to hold back their tears, but they were unsuccessful. Tears started to trickle down their terrified faces.

Sensing that we were ready to leave, Trent reached around his neck and bravely wrapped his trembling fingers around the dog tag that he received the day we met them nearly a year before. It was inscribed with the verse, Jeremiah 29:11. This verse had often comforted him over the past year. He maneuvered it over his head and placed it around my neck as he very confidently asked me to wear it in court. He reminded me that God had a plan. He was absolutely correct. He had often reminded me to trust in God and his plan for our family. His words, in that pivotal moment, transported me from a place of anxiety and fear to that of trust. I held him tight and Mac lifted Mike from the ground to hold him while we uttered one last prayer before heading to the courtroom. Our sheer emotional exhaustion was evidenced by our simple prayer in that moment. Mac offered a prayer of thanks for the time we had spent together and a candid plea for faith in His plan.

Mac's parents who were with us at the beach house created a rapid distraction in order to minimize the emotions as we drove away toward the courthouse. We were ready to stand up

for truth on behalf of Trent and Mike who
had been ours in our hearts from the
day that they walked into our lives.

Ready, Set, Go

As we drove to the courthouse, my demeanor changed from one of sadness and despair to that of strength and power. The last few months had been spent preparing for this moment by gathering data, journaling, meeting with professionals, collecting documentation for court, and mentally preparing to take the stand. I had never been a confrontational person or one who was quick to anger. However, when the well-being and safety of innocent children was at stake, I was prepared to fight. I was not planning to fight physically, but I was prepared to stand strong in the truth and do everything in my power to ensure that the best interests of Mike and Trent would be served. We planned to walk through the front doors of the courtroom with the assurance that we had done everything we could possibly do on behalf of the boys who were not yet legally ours.

We met our attorney in her office for one last briefing. Her powerful confidence was soothing as she escorted us to the courtroom that was going to be our battleground for the next week. We scanned the room for familiar faces and were greeted with a loving smile and a hug from Genevieve who had been the social worker for Trent and Mike for the past two years. She had developed a genuine love for the boys since becoming involved in their case and was prepared to fight on their behalf. We sat patiently toward the back of the courtroom and waited as we watched various unfamiliar parties enter and fill the large room.

We had heard the stories about many of the members of the birth family but had only met Blair (the birth mother) and Cameron (the birth father). Cameron was no longer required to attend the Termination of Parental Rights Hearing since he had relinquished his parental rights three weeks earlier. In the eyes of the law, he was no longer part of the process.

The maternal grandmother, Lilith, had a very negative reputation among the caseworkers and judges. We heard many stories about her past actions. I glanced around the room to see if I could locate her. Then the back door creaked open, and the hair on my arms stood up as an older woman entered the courtroom from the back left. I knew immediately that it was Lilith. She had a terrifying presence that left a very lasting impression. As she entered the room, she sent evil glares our way. We had always treated both Cameron and Blair with kindness and respect. Despite the fact that we had been taking care of her biological grandchildren, we were clearly her target as evidenced by her glares and comments upon entering.

She marched in and immediately demanded time with the attorney that was hired to represent her daughter in the case. I overheard her state that her daughter, Blair, was running late. The judge very patiently addressed the room full of professionals who had traveled from various distances and stated that we would begin once Blair arrived. He had a calm demeanor and appeared to be extremely patient. Blair's attorney, David Blackburn, began to pace back and forth and continually checked his watch as the minutes ticked by. I sat in utter shock as I stared at her empty chair. This was her final chance to come and fight for her children and she was not even present.

The back door of the courtroom slammed open nearly 40 minutes later as an emotionless Blair entered and walked to her attorney with absolutely no apology. Attorney Blackburn nervously approached the judge and reported that Blair was late because she had trouble locating child care for her youngest child who remained with her in the home. With a stern gentleness the judge simply stated, "Let's begin."

The trial began with an introduction of the honorable Judge Ellington. He was very familiar with the history and had been involved in the case from the beginning. Familiar with the possibility of potential outbursts from maternal birth family members, he sternly reminded everyone that we were gathered in the courtroom for one reason and that was to determine what was in the best interest of Trent, Mike and their two siblings.

The dreaded day began with testimony delivered by multiple therapists who had treated the children over the years. Since the Department of Social Services had been involved with this family for many years and the children had been through multiple foster care placements, a large number of therapists who had attempted to deliver services over the years were prepared to testify.

Multiple attorneys were present in the room, and each had their chance to cross examine each key witness. Waiting their turn to draw information to strengthen their side were David Blackburn, the private attorney for Blair; Elizabeth Lancaster, the lawyer for the Department of Social Services; Melissa Porton, the attorney for the Guardian Ad Litem program; and our private attorney, Ann Cunningham.

We quickly realized that this would be painfully lengthy because each attorney was given time to question the witness. However, Mac and I noticed that our attorney did not cross examine the first witness. During the first recess, she guided us to the conference room and explained that she was going to refrain from direct cross examination because having a foster family directly involved on a termination hearing was unprecedented. She wanted to ensure that the birth family had no grounds for an appeal. While she would not cross examine witnesses directly, she would serve as part of the legal team of attorneys that were involved in the questioning. As part of that team, she would be able to guide them without directly questioning the witnesses. Simply having her presence in the room clearly struck fear in the heart of the opposing attorney. Rumor had it that she had defeated him many times in this same courtroom. We had complete faith in our attorney and knew that she was the best in the area. We appreciated her cautious approach to the situation.

After multiple therapists were questioned, the judge called for a rather lengthy recess. Mac and I were informed that the final testimony of the day was going to be given by the woman who initially contacted the Department of Social Services with concerns regarding the children many years earlier. We overheard that she was very frightened to enter the courtroom due to both previous and recent threats from Lilith. We waited patiently as she was given a police escort into the back of the building and kept in a private holding room until it was time for her vital testimony.

The meek woman entered from the back and was escorted to the stand by the bailiff. She was very small in stature and had glasses that hung low on her nose. The woman stared at the ground as she cautiously walked by Lilith. I caught Lilith clearly expressing threatening looks on her face as the brave woman approached to stand in the truth.

As she was sworn in, she visually scanned the room seeming to look for some welcoming faces. We had never met, but I smiled and nodded my head in an effort to show support. She must have determined that we were eager to hear her very important words since her eyes remained fixed on us.

This tiny woman appeared as if she was on the verge of having a panic attack when she began to speak. Her eyes were filled with fear as she looked at the judge and said,"I am really nervous." He thanked her for her presence and asked her to take a minute to breathe before starting. She composed herself, took a deep extended breath and said, "Ok, I am ready."

She vividly described her mounting concern as she watched these dirty and unkempt children wandering the streets unattended in search of food and escape from their current conditions day after day. On several occasions, she attempted to return them home, but the house was empty or Blair refused to come to the door. She lived in close proximity to the family and she often heard screaming and domestic violence coming from their house. The witness described being unable to sleep at night because she was worried about the young children who appeared to need help. Although the opposing attorney attempted to cause her to mis-step in her story, she stood firm and described very clear memories of the repeated events that disturbed her enough to make a report to the Department of Social Services. Her voice shook as she shared every detail she could muster. I felt sickened as her testimony came to a close. The judge saw the fear in her eyes and clearly recognized her cracking voice. He insisted that she receive a police escort out of the back of the building directly to her car. She stepped down from the stress of the witness stand and glanced over the crowd with fear in her eyes. In that moment, we were very thankful for her bravery many years earlier and for her willingness to stand in the courtroom and share the truth. She stood and spoke for the children despite her deep-seeded fear of repercussions.

We purposely waited until the courtroom cleared before exiting with our attorney who walked us back to her office to talk about her impressions of the day. We remained fixated on her words as she told us that everything had gone as planned and that the more important testimonies were scheduled for the days ahead. I had a deep desire for her to look me in the eye and tell me that everything was going to be fine, but she was unable to do that; too much unknown remained. She instructed us to return home and hug our boys and get some much-needed sleep to prepare for a very emotionally trying day ahead.

Blair was scheduled to testify the next day.

Running on Empty

Motherhood is not a gift that is bestowed on everyone. In my opinion, being granted the job of caring for a young life should be viewed as one of the most important tasks in a woman's life.

Over the previous year, I was blessed with the gift of two young boys who had experienced more trauma and heartache than I ever imagined feasible. We opened our hearts from the moment they entered our home and embraced our role as parents even though it was not official in the eyes of the law. We proved, over time, that we were going to provide for their basic needs, keep them safe, and love them as a mother and father should. Even if our time with them was going to come to an end, I had been able to help two boys feel loved and truly cherished for the first time in their lives.

I was raised by an amazing woman who stood by my side each and every day. She was present to cheer me on at every milestone and to wrap her arms around me in times of sadness. My dad, always offered a source of quiet strength and showed support that never waivered. As a child, I woke each morning knowing that no matter what came my way, my parents would be by my side. Even into adulthood, my parents offered unconditional love and support.

Just as she had done many times when I was young, my mom grasped my hand as we entered the cramped elevator of the courtroom. We both took a deep breath as the unspoken fears and anxiety crept into our thoughts. We both knew that we had a very emotionally difficult day ahead.

We were smacked in the face with heat and humidity as we opened the courtroom door for day two of testimony. The air conditioning was clearly not functioning properly as evidenced by the sweat pouring down the faces of those who had entered before us. Within minutes we felt sweat begin to drip from our foreheads. The unexpected heat worsened what was already an unpleasant and uncomfortable setting.

Many birth family members entered the room in support of Blair. The entire day was reserved for her testimony and cross examination. Even though we were only in day two, I had learned the players in this game and watched various groups of people whispering and glaring across the courtroom.

The paternal grandparents, Cameron's mom and dad, entered the courtroom about ten minutes prior to start time and approached us with a welcoming and warm smile. Uncertain where they stood on the issues at hand, we cautiously engaged them in a conversation. Their body language and warm conversation sent the message that they were in support of doing what was in the best interest of the children. Their son had already relinquished his parental rights, and they were in attendance to ensure that justice was being served for the four children whom they loved. They moved their items and sat directly behind us. Their blatant move sent a clear message of camaraderie to the maternal side of the family. Immediately upon their move to our side of the courtroom, the maternal side of the birth family began gathering in a group, whispering, and pointing. They were very visibly upset by the choice made by the paternal grandparents.

As our 9:00 a.m. start time approached, we rose to a stand to show respect to the honorable judge who entered from the back and said, "Good morning." Attorney Blackburn had a clear look of distress as he began to pace and share glances between his phone, watch, and the back door of the courtroom. Just like the previous day, Blair had not arrived in the courtroom at the appointed time. This tardiness was even more disturbing than the first day because this was the day set aside for her to speak to the judge about her desire to have her children returned to her. Nearly 40 minutes passed and Attorney Blackburn approached other birth family members asking if they had heard from Blair with an explanation about why she was late.

I began to get agitated as I saw my own mother, who was there to support me, become uncomfortable with the elevated temperature in the room. She had been diagnosed with fibromyalgia many years earlier and was not able to tolerate the heat due to her disease. Becoming concerned, I asked her if she needed to leave and head back to the beach house. As soon as the words left my lips, she immediately and clearly expressed that she would not even consider being separated from me in my time of need. Once again, she put my needs ahead of her own.

My mom's firm commitment to me made me feel deep sadness for my boys. Not only did Blair have a history of putting her needs ahead of her children, but she wasn't even able to make it to a life-altering court hearing in a timely manner to fight for their return to her. Her opportunity to testify was her chance to plead with the judge and make her desires known. Part of me hoped that I would hear emotional words come from her mouth. I needed to believe that she had a desperate longing to be reunited with the children to whom she had given birth. I wanted to believe that the boys had occasionally felt love and affection from her. I loved them too much to think that they lived the early years of their lives without the basic nurturing that every child deserves.

I placed my headphones in my ears and played my calming Christian music as the moments ticked away. The music kept me grounded and kept my anger at a dull roar.

At 10:20, 1 hour and 20 minutes past our scheduled court time, Blair entered the courtroom and slowly meandered up to her attorney who was clearly upset by her lack of actions and timeliness. When asked where she had been, she nonchalantly reported that she had been unable to locate her keys. She delivered no apology, showed no emotion, and clearly had no understanding of how she had impacted those around her. I was clearly able to see some of the characteristics associated with her diagnosed disorders. The judge responded with a rather sarcastic, "Well, we are glad you decided to join us."

I had prepared myself emotionally for this day through prayer and other calming techniques, but we were starting the day 1 hour and 20 minutes late, and we were already saturated in sweat. I took a quick walk to the restroom to compose myself and wipe some of the sweat from my face. As I glanced in the mirror, I saw the dog tag Trent had given me and was reminded that God was in control. All the aggravation was pushed aside as I developed laser-like focus. I was ready to begin the day.

Back in the courtroom, Blair gripped her Bible as she was called to the stand. She entered the elevated box and placed the sacred book by her side in an obvious attempt to impress the judge. As a strong Christian, I swallowed hard as I saw someone who had severely neglected her children, had exhibited daily domestic violence, and had willingly allowed continual sexual abuse to occur, misuse God's word. Within moments, she had proven that carrying the Bible was nothing more than a show. The judge was wise and saw through the facade. Immediately after she had sworn to tell the truth while on the stand, he questioned her about her knowledge of the Bible and her church attendance. After only a few sentences, he quickly had Blair admitting that she had not read the Bible or attended church for over ten years. He made a point to let her know that he understood her act as an attempt to influence him.

One attorney after another questioned Blair about her past actions, her awareness of past abuse, and her ability to parent the children if they were to return to her. I truly cannot find the words to describe her lack of emotion in every response that was delivered. I longed to hear her describe her love for her children and her desire to have them return to her. Despite a tremendous amount of coaching and preparation with her attorney, not one time in seven hours of testimony did she say that she loved her children. Not a single word involving emotion was delivered. She stared blankly into space and very frequently responded with "I don't know" or "I can't remember" when extremely important questions were fired her way.

After the initial questioning, Blair spoke directly to the judge about what a wonderful childhood she had provided for her children. She delivered lie after lie about the meals she had prepared, the time she had spent with them, the homework help she had given them, and other clearly rehearsed responses. I began to feel extremely disturbed as I noticed that even the rehearsed responses remained emotionless.

The restraint required by me to remain seated and listen to her lie under oath is indescribable. My anger was building, not because of what she had done to me, but because of what she had done to the boys I had come to love so deeply. I could have dredged up some compassion if she had been willing to admit wrongdoing or show even the slightest bit of remorse. Instead, her approach was to say that she had provided a perfect childhood and the Department of Social Services had wrongly removed her children. She also claimed to have no mental illness and no need for therapy. I almost bit a hole through my lip in an effort to remain quiet as she spoke. I knew that I would be afforded my time to speak at some point in the trial, but I had to use all of the emotional strength within me not to jump up and shout the truth in those moments.

Until that day in court, I had never before been angered to the point of tears. That is a feeling I will never forget. On multiple occasions throughout her hellacious testimony, I was so overcome with a combination of anger and heartache on behalf of Trent and Mike that I was forced to remove myself from the courtroom. I needed to regulate my emotions that were about to cause me to implode. I frequently stepped out and moved into a bathroom stall to cry and release some emotion before returning to the infuriating trial. Blair had been given the gift of beautiful children, and she had failed them.

I had always struggled to comprehend the fact that both Mike and Trent claimed to have very little emotional connection to her. However, based on her responses in the courtroom, I was able to see how that was most certainly a reality. She was truly emotionless and maintained a blank stare during what should have been an emotion-laden testimony. I felt deep pain as I looked at her and saw the evidence of her hollow existence. I fluctuated between feelings of empathy sheer anger because she was so clearly out of touch with reality. She had hurt her children by her unwillingness to accept the services that had been offered over many years.

I gripped my own hand so tight that my fingernails were starting to rip the skin in the center of my palm. I gripped harder with every lie that was told. The majority of the lies were exposed as the attorneys easily confused her and her story changed repeatedly. Each time she knew she was trapped, she responded with "I don't recall." Her attorney was obviously disenchanted with her as he rolled his eyes each time she was unable to respond.

While her whole testimony pointed to abuse and neglect of the children she had birthed, the most damaging to her case were the following untrue reports from her. First, she claimed that she was happily married to Cameron. Second, she said that together they provided two incomes to support the children. Third, she spoke of a house where they lived that would provide sufficient space for the children if they returned to live with them. These were a few of the criteria that needed to be met in order for the children to return.

We had been in contact with Cameron, the birth father, on a frequent basis and knew that he was leaving Blair and moving to Louisiana. The truth relating to those vital details needed to be exposed, but since Cameron was under no obligation to attend court, we were uncertain as to how that was going to occur.

Within a few short moments, Blair had proven the she did not have a realistic understanding of the situation. She had received reports about the boys time in therapy during their time in foster care. These reports proved that the boys had severe trauma as a result of time spent in her home. Yet, she adamantly claimed that they had an ideal childhood. With complete apathy, she claimed that she too, had been abused as a child and that she was simply able to "get over it" with no help. She felt that the children she had birthed should do the same.

In spite of the fact that Blair had been diagnosed by multiple professionals with Histrionic Personality Disorder, Narcissistic Personality Disorder, and other disorders, she claimed to have no mental illness. Multiple reports from psychological evaluations were presented and all but one concurred with the collection of diagnosis from the DSM which is the official criteria for diagnosing mental disorders.

As afternoon approached, everyone in the courtroom became convinced that this court battle was initiated by Lilith. She was unable to control herself as she repeatedly approached Blair's attorney and barked direct orders on how to respond in front of the judge. She was clearly enraged when she felt he was not doing an adequate job. After repeated outbursts, Lilith had exposed herself as the ring-leader of this highly dysfunctional family.

As the emotionally painful day came to a close, many emotions rushed around inside my head. Although I faced a lot of anger, the overwhelming emotion was sadness. I felt a deep pain from sitting through seven hours of testimony without seeing a single tear shed by the woman who gave birth to Trent and Mike. She never stated that she wanted them to return to her.

Blair had spent the day in court doing what her mother, Lilith, had asked her to do to prove that she could care for the children. However, not once during her seven hours of emotionless testimony did she state that she wanted the children to return to her. More than ever before, I wanted to race back home to Trent and Mike and tell them how much we loved them. I wanted them to never doubt again that they were absolutely precious and deserved happiness.

Seeing Blair up close and personal for seven hours helped me truly understand how extremely emotionally neglected they had been.

Utterly exhausted and in desperate need of a shower from a long day of sweating, we entered the beach house and gripped both boys tightly while we told them how much we loved them. Visions of Blair's unemotional face flashed in my head as I clung onto my boys. Never again would I allow them to have any question about how much they are loved.

Trent and Mike clung to us as they desperately asked how our day had gone. Trent eagerly asked, "Did the judge say yes to adoption?" They looked deeply disappointed when we told them that we had to wait longer.

The day had been long and we had very little energy, so we sat on the porch as a family and listened to the waves without speaking. I simply watched the waves roll in and out as I rehashed the events of the day. Within the next few days, the uncertainty would end, one way or another.

I reached down and ran my finger over the engraved words on the dog tag that Trent had given me to wear into the courtroom and reminded myself of God's plan. As the verse stated, "For I know the plans I have for you declares the Lord, plans to prosper you and not to harm you, plans to give you hope and a future". Later that night, I held onto hope as I closed my eyes after the most trying day of my life, a hope of a future with my family, hope that we would be a legal family in the eyes of the law within a few short days.

One Single Post It Note

As each day in court passed, less people were present to support Blair and Lilith. Their support dwindled as the truth unfolded.

On day three, the morning hours were filled with continued testimony from social workers, additional therapists and others involved in the case. All of them claimed that Blair was unable or unwilling to keep her children safe. They also confirmed that she was unwilling to work toward making the needed changes required by the court. After a few hours of rather uneventful testimony, we took a recess for lunch.

During lunch, our attorney briefed us on what was scheduled to take place during the afternoon hours. Sounding concerned, she reported that Lilith had located a therapist who had evaluated Blair and was attempting to prove that the multiple mental illness diagnosis were untrue and inaccurate. This was somewhat concerning since her testimony would potentially unravel everything we had spent the past two days proving. My anxiety started to increase as I saw concern on the faces of the attorneys and social workers involved. The confidence and assurance was gone from their voices. I reached down and grasped the dog tag around my neck as a symbolic reminder that God was in control.

After the lunch break, Beth O'hair, a licensed therapist, swore to tell the truth and took her place in the witness stand. She was dressed professionally and appeared to be well educated in the field. The first two hours were devoted to the therapist being questioned by Blair's attorney. The line of repetitive questioning was clearly designed to prove that Blair had been misdiagnosed with Histrionic Personality Disorder, a disorder that would make parenting extremely challenging. Therapy notes were examined and used as proof that the disorder did not exist. These therapy notes disagreed with three other professionals that had previously diagnosed the Axis III disorder. Although Blair typically showed minimal emotion which is not one of the factors involved in this disorder, evidence was clearly presented from other multiple therapists that she, without question, met the criteria for the diagnosis. After multiple hours, Attorney Blackburn proudly rested his case and clearly felt confident that he had done his job to prove Blair as a fit mother.

I fearfully glanced at our attorney who had been carefully analyzing the situation for over two hours. Since she was unable to directly cross examine the witness, she calmly passed the D.S.S. Attorney a single post-it-note. Out of extreme curiosity, I tried to read it but could not make out the scribbled words.

The D.S.S. Attorney smirked before she approached the therapist to cross-examine. She walked as close to the supposed professional as possible and stated words I will never forget, "I simply have 2 questions for you." She allowed a long dramatic pause to build suspense before asking the first damaging question, "Can you please give me the medical definition of Histrionic Personality Disorder?" The therapist looked around the room with a sense of panic that turned to defeat and after a lengthy moment of silence responded with the damaging words, "No, I am sorry. I cannot."

Multiple gasps were heard around the room. The opposing legal team had just spent the last two hours proving that Blair did not have Histrionic Personality Disorder when the professional who made that claim could not even define the disorder she had been refuting. With one single post it note offered by our attorney, the opposing counsel had just taken a deep and damaging blow.

The D.S.S. Attorney continued with her second question, "Lastly, how many other clients have you treated with this disorder?" Again with a look of total disbelief and utter defeat the therapist stated, "None - Blair was my first and only." The D.S.S. Attorney proudly turned to the judge with a large smile on her face and calmly stated, "I have no further questions for the witness."

Deafening silence spread across the room as the realization sank in that if the therapist had very minimal understanding of the disorder she had been attempting to refute.

The team of attorneys working on behalf of the boys had masterfully destroyed two hours of very detailed testimony with two single questions scribbled on a single post-it-note. All credibility established by the opposing attorney was lost with those two simple questions.

We felt good about the team of people who were representing our children in court. In addition, we knew that we had an entire support system back home praying and sending us e-mails and texts. We knew that our friends were ready to support us no matter the outcome. In spite of this strong support system, fear and doubt still crept into our minds.

We only had one last large hurdle to jump. The judge was still of the understanding that Cameron was contributing to the income and would help raise the children alongside Blair if they returned home. Once again, we met with the attorney at the end of the day. She appeared somewhat concerned about the situation. She suggested that we call Cameron and ask him to come in to court and do what was in the best interest of his children. Knowing that he was fearful of the maternal side of the family after relinquishing his rights without telling them, the attorneys doubted that he would voluntarily face them directly in the courtroom.

The social worker, attorneys, and others had already attempted to persuade Cameron to come to court the following day but were unsuccessful since he was not legally bound to do so. The legal team threatened to subpoena him, but they explained that it would slow the entire process significantly and the boys would then linger in uncertainty even longer.

That night, after much prayer, Mac decided to step away and call Cameron. They had a heartfelt conversation. Mac explained that Cameron needed to do this for his children so that they would be able to find true happiness. Mac also explained that he was eventually going to be forced to enter the courtroom because his testimony was required in order to dispel the lies that were being told by Blair.

After much conversation and coaxing, Cameron agreed to attend court the next morning in order to testify that he had signed his rights away and that he was planning to leave Blair and move to another state. Mac assured him that he was making the right decision and thanked him for putting his children first in this case.

Every time we interacted with Cameron, he was very fearful. For that reason, we were extremely concerned that he would change his mind and choose not to appear in the courtroom the next morning. We prayed that night that he would have the strength to face his fears and speak the truth. Only time would tell.

Is This the Jerry Springer Show?

Never in my wildest dreams did I ever imagine that I would be in a courtroom witnessing actions that could have easily landed us in an episode of the Jerry Springer Show. We entered day four knowing that drama was likely to unfold since Cameron was scheduled to take the stand and tell the truth about his intentions. What actually unfolded was beyond any chaos that I ever imagined possible.

Immediately upon entering the courtroom, which thankfully had a functioning air conditioner again, we were briefed and told that Cameron was scheduled to testify first. We also learned that Lilith had somehow uncovered his plan overnight and had issued threats to keep him from speaking. Uncertain about whether Cameron was aware of the threats, Mac decided to text him and arrange to escort him into the building. Despite the fact that he is one of the most soft-hearted people I know, Mac was a very muscular and had a very intimidating presence. We were fairly certain that the maternal birth family would not try to harm Cameron if Mac was with him.

We were very relieved once Mac received the much anticipated text saying that Cameron had arrived. Mac exited the building, escorted Cameron to the courtroom, and guided him to a seat with his parents directly behind us. That was a very surreal moment. At one time, we had vowed to never even meet the birth family face to face, so Mac escorting the birth father into the building was an ironic twist to the story.

The tension in the room was palpable. Knowing that Lilith called the shots, I continued to watch her actions as I attempted to predict her future moves.

Cameron timidly approached the stand and began to face a barrage of questions that slowly exposed the truth. He faced his fears and spoke the truth regarding Blair's ability to parent and shared his plans to leave her and relocate to another state. I kept my eyes fixed on Blair, assuming that she would show signs of devastation as she learned publicly that she was losing her husband, her house, and potentially her children. Frighteningly, she showed no change in her demeanor whatsoever. I was astounded at her ability to tune out emotional pain and appear as though nothing had happened. Every bit of her life was crumbling, but she had no response. Lilith, however, was enraged and clearly had her sights set on Cameron.

After Cameron finished his testimony, the social worker asked Mac if he would escort Cameron out of the building. I glared at Lilith across the courtroom to be sure she understood that I was watching her every move. She frightened many, but she did not frighten me anymore. I knew that I had the truth on my side, and I did not fear.

As Cameron's testimony closed, Lilith stood up to move to the hall in an attempt to corner him. After Lilith made her move, the judge decided to remove Cameron by police escort out the back door in order to ensure safety for all. I headed into the hall to observe her actions. When the door opened, Lilith expected to see her previous son-in-law. Instead, she looked face to face with me. I knew she had been asked to leave the courtroom during previous hearings due to aggressive behavior, so I fully expected her to approach. Lilith clearly knew that I was not afraid and was not going to be intimidated by her threats. She quickly looked away from my very evident glare and returned to the courtroom to scold their attorney yet again.

We had only one more day of testimonies before the judge was scheduled to make his final ruling in the Termination of Parental Rights phase of the hearing. I knew that my turn was approaching. I had never been so ready to stand in front of a courtroom and speak the truth for the two boys who needed me to fight on their behalf.

My Turn

On the days leading up to my testimony, I had experienced anxiety. However, four days filled with lies without the ability to speak the truth had removed that fear. An extreme eagerness to speak and reveal the full, real story had replaced the fear. I reveled in the fact that I could finally be a voice for my boys.

I took the stand as an expert witness in behavior management and child development. I was instructed before taking the stand that I was not able to speak freely; I was only permitted to answer the questions that were asked of me by the various attorneys. Having had four days to study the opposing attorney, I felt prepared for his attack and was ready to remain steps ahead of him in order to guide the questioning in the direction that I desired.

When they called my name, I gripped Mac's hand one last time and tucked the dog tag in my dress before approaching the bench. My heart was racing and my hands were trembling, but it was not from fear. The reaction stemmed from a formidable desire to speak for my boys who were too young to have a voice of their own in the courtroom. I was prepared with files filled with elaborate behavioral data that had been tracked and graphed. This data indicated a clear spike in misbehaviors when Trent and Mike had an increased fear of leaving our home.

I was first questioned by the D.S.S. and GAL attorneys who led the questions to show the data indicating a definite change in behavior when the boys faced a fear of loss. While the lawyers never spoke the words that the boys wanted to remain with our family, the data pointed to those ideas. I was extremely careful to remain professional and not express too much emotion during my testimony.

Attorney Blackburn seemed to be eager to get his turn with me. He stared me directly in the face with a smug look as he paced back and forth in front of the stand. I was well prepared for his intimidation tactics as he began throwing various questions at me regarding my credentials. I was prepared for this line of questioning and immediately provided him with a paper copy of all of my diplomas, certifications, and recognitions within the field. He was provided with an extensive list of awards and recognitions in addition to several additional areas of certification. That line of questioning quickly ended as he sifted through the stack of certifications, honors, and awards. He seemed to realize that he would be unable to attack me professionally, so he shifted to a personal attack.

The attorney's next approach involved the false theory that Mac and I were desperate for children due to infertility and that I fabricated data in order to meet that goal. He obviously had not done his research. He began asking questions about the thousands of dollars we had spent on infertility treatments. That line of questioning quickly came to a rapid halt as he learned that we had planned to adopt since the age of sixteen and had never once sought infertility treatment.

Attorney Blackburn was visibly rattled by my quick and confident responses and his inability to lead my answers. I carefully crafted my answers in order to set up his next question. I desperately wanted to be able to talk about Trent and Mike's desire to be adopted, but could only do so if a line of questioning opened that door. I slowly and methodically led the conversation in that direction and hoped that Attorney Blackburn would follow.

My plan worked beautifully as he led me down a line of questioning that opened up topics I hoped would be addressed. He stumbled on his words and hurdled questions wanting to know if the boys had expressed a desire to return home to their birth family. With that one question, I pounced and was able to provide journal writings, letters to the judge written by the boys, and a folder full of other evidence that otherwise would not have been submitted.

I felt extremely strong and empowered on the stand. I effectively channeled all of the emotion that had been building over the past year into that one moment when I was given the opportunity to advocate for my boys. Attorney Blackburn soon realized that he had opened lines of questioning that he needed to close quickly, and he began objecting to nearly every comment that left my mouth. He objected so frequently that it became humorous. He clearly had nowhere left to turn.

Not only was this attorney unable to break me down, my ability to manipulate his questioning enabled me to speak the truth and share much needed information with the judge.

When I stepped down from the stand my adrenaline was pumping, and I was very proud of myself for speaking the truth! The other attorneys immediately praised me for my strength and my very powerful testimony. That moment felt amazing; I had given my boys a voice.

After my testimony, we broke for a recess. After lunch we were scheduled to hear from one remaining witness before the verdict was going to be delivered. We were nearing the time for the most crucial decision of our lives to be made.

Stand Off

Knowing that the verdict was drawing near stole my appetite. During lunch, I questioned the attorney about the last remaining witness because I felt that everyone had already testified. She explained that this witness had not been scheduled to attend, but the opposing attorney insisted at the demand of Lilith. She then shared that Travis, Trent and Mike's older brother, had a right to testify and express his opinion about adoption since he was over the age of twelve. He had submitted an official testimony in writing to the judge in order to avoid the need to face his birth family directly. Keeping the best interest of Travis in mind, the judge agreed that the written document could serve as his testimony. However, Lilith insisted that the writing had been falsified and demanded that Travis enter the courtroom and make his testimony in person. The judge, social workers, and even the opposing counsel expressed concern and pleaded with them not to require this of a thriteen-year-old boy who had already experienced enough pain. Despite the pleas, they insisted that he enter the courtroom, convinced that he had been forced to write his testimony letter. Phone calls were made and his adoptive parent was scheduled to bring him into the courtroom.

The previous days in the courtroom had taught me to be hyper-vigilant about what was happening around me. I kept my eyes fixed on Lilith and listened carefully to catch the words she spoke. My careful attention paid well. I heard her say with anger on her face that she was planning to catch Travis in the parking lot before they got into the courtroom so she could talk to him before he spoke to the judge. I shared this information with the social worker who immediately began making alternate plans to bring him in through the judges chambers by police escort.

Knowing that this case was nearing an end seemed to increase the desperation and anger on Lilith's face. Travis was not living in our home; he was going to be adopted by another family. However, I had no intention of allowing Lilith to traumatize him further.

After a few short moments, the judge stated, "Travis has arrived and will be up shortly." Lilith rose to her feet, opened the back door of the courtroom and headed quickly for the elevator in her last ditch attempt to manipulate the family she had controlled for so long. The second I saw her stand, I acted instinctively and rushed to the elevator to make it clear that I knew her intentions. No words were spoken, and no one else was near. I simply took a very strong stance in front of the elevator door which was her only way to make it down to Travis in time to catch him. I had my back to the elevator door and did not push any buttons. I silently stared at her as she began to get angry. She tried to move around me, and I moved in her path, clearly indicating that I was not letting her onto that elevator. I realized that this was a risky move, but because a child needed protection, I was willing to take the risk. We exchanged several very uncomfortable glances before she paused and looked me deeply in the eyes. I did not waiver and stared her down until she must have realized that I was not moving. Lilith then rapidly headed off to look for the stairs in the corner of the building, but I knew it was too late; they had already brought Travis up the back entrance and into the judges quarters.

The next hour was spent with closed door conversations between the judge, Travis and Blair. Much to her displeasure, Lilith was not permitted to enter, so she paced nervously back and forth in the back of the courtroom.

Eventually the door creaked open. I first saw the smiling face of the social worker, Genevieve, followed by Travis who took a run down the aisle of the courtroom and climbed into his pre-adoptive mother's lap. Travis had obviously found the strength to express his desire to be adopted, despite being forced to face his birth mother directly across a table. The court was called to order, and we were informed that the judge was resigning to his quarters. He would return soon with a decision about the Termination of Parental Rights.

As I watched the honorable judge close the door to his chambers, I prayed that he had heard the truth and would make the decision to allow the children happiness for the first time in their existence. I also prayed a heartfelt prayer that I would accept whatever the

verdict may be. I trusted God's plan.
Trent and Mike belonged to Him.

The Verdict

Every ounce of fear and doubt returned as we watched the judge enter his chambers for the final time. My vision narrowed and became clouded as I attempted to grasp the reality that the decision was approaching. Mac, Mom, and I bowed our heads for a final prayer as we waited to hear the words that would determine the rest of our lives. I glanced one last time at the dog tag and remembered Trent's words about our need to trust God. We had already given Trent and Mike our hearts and wanted more than anything to be able to deliver the news that they no longer needed to live in fear. We dreamed of wrapping our arms around them and telling them that they were going to be part of our family forever.

Thirty minutes later Mac pulled me close as the judge re-entered the courtroom and moved into his chair. I had been with Mac since we were 16 years old and had never seen him frightened until this moment. He had never exhibited fear of physical pain, but the fear of losing his boys was agonizingly real. I felt his heartbeat increase as I leaned against him; it felt like it was going to pound out of his chest. I gripped his hand.

With one final tap of the gavel the judge stated, "Parental rights have been terminated." Time froze and I wanted to hear him repeat the words over and over. I looked at Mac and said, "What did he say?" I sat stunned in utter disbelief as the tears began to flow down my cheeks. It was finished. Mac and I clung to one another with our shaking hands as the reality sank in that this battle was complete. Over 12 months of fear, uncertainty, sadness, and anger dissipated with those few words uttered by the judge.

Lilith could no longer control her anger. As my Mom and our friend, Kathy, embraced in a quiet celebratory hug, Lilith approached my mom from behind and reached for her in an angry rage. The bailiff quickly intervened and forcibly moved Lilith to the far wall and kept her there until we gathered our belongings.

After the drama at the conclusion of the Termination of Parental Rights portion of the hearing, the judge decided that we required a police escort to our vehicles. As the bailiff escorted us down the darkened hall, she glanced our way, grasped the taser at her belt and said, "You know, you can't fix stupid, but you sure can taser it". We all laughed at the statement that was exactly what we needed to take the edge off of the overwhelming emotions. As we exited the building, we felt tremendous relief in knowing that we had just one more day in court to complete the "Best Interest" phase. We could then head home to begin our life as a family of four.

On the drive home, all we talked about was the fact that we were only moments away from delivering the ultimate good news to Trent and Mike. Mac and I jokingly argued about which one of us was going to say the words they longed to hear. We speculated and looked forward to seeing and hearing how they would react. Mac lovingly said he would allow me the pleasure of delivering the verdict.

Although the verdict had been delivered, my body was aching from muscle tension and the constant state of stress we had endured over the past week. I was hopeful that I would begin to relax after I told our boys that they were going to be ours forever. No words could be sweeter than the words I prepared to speak to our boys.

As we approached the beach house, I barely waited for Mac to park before I opened my car door to rush in to the boys who had eagerly awaited for word each day. We were finally able to deliver the words that they had so desperately wanted to hear for over a year.

I entered the house and walked up the long steps to locate Trent and Mike. I found them playing a game at the table. Rather than share the information in front of a crowd, I asked them to follow me to one of the nearby bedrooms. I tried to hide my bursting enthusiasm until we were alone as a family, but it was extremely difficult to curtail. We crossed into the bedroom and they were consumed with a concerned look in their emotion-filled eyes. I looked at them and enthusiastically screamed, "The judge said yes."

I wish I had videotaped the celebration that ensued. The rules we worked so hard to instill were forgotten as they launched into shouts of joy, jumped up and down on the bed and ran around the room in a chaotic and crazy celebration of freedom from their past. The chains were gone. Until that day, this moment had only been a dream. Finally it was a reality.

We embraced in a family hug and repeated the words, "We are going to be a forever family." We dropped to our knees in a prayer of thanks, and Trent said, "See Mom, I told you God had a plan." We had been full of worry for so long that it was difficult to fathom the reality of the verdict. We slept with a complete and total sense of peace that night as we rested up for one final day in court.

Best Interest

Although we heard the words we longed to hear from the judge regarding the Termination of Parental Rights, we still needed to spend one last day in court to complete the Best Interest phase of the trial. This final phase was to determine if adoption was in the best interest of the children.

Trent and Mike had been thriving since being in our care. Because they had made such tremendous progress, our attorney felt that this portion of the process was a mere technicality. During this phase of the trial, both Mac and I would both be given an opportunity to take the stand and state our intentions to adopt the boys we already considered ours.

We entered the courtroom on the final day with a complete sense of peace in knowing that the boys were now free for adoption. As we looked around the courtroom, only five birth family members remained: Blair, Lilith, Blair's brother and sister-in-law, and one family friend. Although I was angry at her for all she had needlessly put us through over the past week, I felt deep empathy for Blair because she had lost her home, her husband, and her children all within a span of four days. I was determined to show her God's love through my actions and planned to speak directly to her and comfort her as this case came to a close.

We looked forward to the opportunity to share our feelings and intentions with the judge. During this phase, we were permitted to share our data, pictures, and documentation that demonstrated the progress the boys had made over the past year.

I was called to the stand for the second and final time. This time, my presence was brief as I passionately stated my desire to adopt both Trent and Mike.

Mac was prepared to do the majority of the presentation and had a very detailed presentation prepared. As he connected various cords and wires in preparation for his slideshow, I felt a strong desire to move up front and sit next to Blair in an effort to show empathy for her as she prepared to watch a depiction of her children who were thriving and happy under the care of another family. I imagined that this would be the most painful moment of her existence. I moved to the seat directly next to her.

As the lights dimmed, Mac began presenting our progress, services we had put in place, and experiences we had provided. Most impactful were a number of quotes from both boys regarding their happiness in our home as well as a large collection of pictures illustrating their love toward us through hugs, smiles, and other joyous moments. The presentation confirmed that we had been functioning as a loving family, despite the fact that the courts had not finalized it. The judge was emotionally moved by Mac's presentation; he wiped tears from his eyes. He said that he could clearly see that the boys were happy and thriving in our care and thanked us for our commitment and dedication to the children. Tears formed in the eyes of the social workers, guardian's ad litem, and attorneys as they realized how much we truly loved and were committed to Trent and Mike.

While pictures of our unofficial family of four scrolled by on the large screen, I sat directly next to Blair waiting for the perfect moment to deliver my words of comfort. I planned to show her love and compassion in her darkest hour. I watched and waited for the moment that she appeared to be overcome with sadness. However, that moment never came. She watched the pictures scroll by and sat emotionless. This was the same demeanor she had maintained throughout the entire trial. My heart broke one last time for her as I realized in that moment that she must have had a tremendous amount of unresolved trauma from her own past, significant enough trauma that she was no longer able to show emotion. At one point I put my arm on her shoulder and said, "This must be very hard for you; I am so sorry". That was one of the most difficult moments of my life as I put my anger aside to show compassion for the woman who had so deeply hurt the boys I was going to raise as my own. She sat silently and motionless as the presentation continued.

Everyone in the room watched the presentation with the exception of Lilith who turned her body and refused to look. She spoke inaudible words of protest as well as statements about getting the boys back when they turned eighteen. As I watched her lay of reaction, I felt true compassion for her as well. She appeared to be facing significant mental illness and was in complete denial about the finality of what had happened in the courtroom.

As Mac completed his presentation and the lights came back up, the room was filled with emotion. The judge did not wait long until he concluded this portion of the trial with a very clear desire for the boys to be adopted by our family. God's plan had come to fruition and the roller coaster ride was finally over. While those were the words we expected to hear, we felt an overwhelming sense of relief to actually hear the words coming from his lips.

As we exited the courthouse and walked down the path that was lined by beautiful historic oak trees, we were overwhelmed with joy. We knew that we would see this building one more time, but that day would be a joyous celebration of a finalized adoption.

The Final Stamp

A few months passed and we began to settle in as a family unit and learn how to function without the constant stress and worry that had been our norm before the court sessions. We knew that the rest of the process would take time. We impatiently awaited the call with an invitation to the courthouse one more time to finalize the adoption.

One day my phone rang. I glanced at the incoming number on my cell phone and saw that Mac was calling. He typically called at least once a day to check on the family and express his love since he had long hours at work. In a frantic voice, he told me that we would be finalizing the adoption the very next morning at the same courthouse that had been a source of tremendous stress and chaos a few months earlier. We were already functioning like a family, but each of us craved the finality of the official adoption decree.

As I delivered the news to the boys, the excitement set in and they immediately began to make preparations for the very special day ahead. I quickly informed my family and friends to see who could join us for the momentous occasion that would occur in under 24 hours. After a quick trip to the mall, we each set out our outfits that would be worn to court to mark the official formation of Team Taylor.

The next morning as we drove through their birthplace for the final time, we all felt differently than we had on previous trips. We drove the familiar roads and passed visual reminders of their pain. This time we were simply traveling through a part of their past with a specific destination in mind. We talked about the fact that this would be the last trip on this road unless they chose to return later in life.

We arrived at the courthouse on a beautiful, sunny autumn morning and recognized the tall trees that had clearly been growing for hundreds of years. They had changed color and were starting to drop their leaves. As I viewed the courthouse, I couldn't help but recall all the emotions it had evoked several months ago. I was forced to remind myself that we were arriving there for a very different purpose.

As we exited the car with my parents and two family friends, Laura Buscher and Isaac Gomez, Genevieve was waiting with a welcoming smile, balloons, and a picture of her with the boys. We were so extremely grateful for her true dedication and commitment to Trent and Mike through this painful process. She had to say goodbye as they finalized their lives with us. Tears filled her eyes as we snapped a few photos before entering the courtroom for the final time.

We entered the building and sat on an old creaky bench. The room was small and filled with antique furniture. We heard footsteps and waited for the clerk to round the corner. She greeted us with a welcoming smile and asked us to follow her. We entered a small conference room and sat to await instructions. With the Clerk of Courts, we signed the necessary paperwork and only had one step remaining before the long awaited adoption would be complete.

Mike used all of his might to pull down the lever to stamp his adoption decree. Mac needed to help him as he pressed the seal into the paper that would forever declare us a family in the eyes of the law. Shortly after, Trent slammed the seal into the document with an unmistakable smile on his face. I watched each adoption decree receive the legal and binding seal. I was so full of love, peace, and joy and thanked God for the journey that had been filled with extreme pain, but had shaped each of us in the process. We were stronger as individuals and most certainly stronger as a family unit.

We left with smiles plastered on our faces as we gripped the legal documents that declared the words we had longed to hear for nearly eighteen months.

As the courthouse faded away in the rearview mirror, I shook my head in disbelief at what had happened in that building. I left a of piece of me there. I had poured every ounce of my heart and soul into the battle that set our children free. What happened behind those walls was now part of our family history. We were headed home to begin our life together as the family that God intended. At the same time, I said a silent prayer for the birth family members. I prayed that they would find peace and healing.

<u>Healing</u>

Healing is never easy. Just as physical wounds hurt worse as they begin to heal, so do emotional wounds. A person must feel the pain at its greatest intensity in order to move beyond it and allow healing to occur.

Now that we no longer had to focus every ounce of energy on the fear of losing our family, we were able to start focusing on true healing for the boys who had simply been in a fight or flight response for the past eighteen months.

Doors were no longer being locked incessantly, conversations were no longer fixated on court, and the boys began to feel safe in their home. Once that general sense of safety was instilled, we were able to begin healing as a family.

Admitting that the process had taken an extreme toll on us was difficult. The truth could not be denied. The boys were not the only ones who had suffered through the whole ordeal of the past eighteen months. Mac and I had also been impacted. Despite the fact that the abuse did not occur directly to us, compassion fatigue and secondary trauma are very real. We were exhausted, but we knew that Trent and Mike had a significant amount of healing ahead.

Over time, we began to view the challenges as a gift. We worked together on ways to enjoy the challenges that we knew were ahead. We taught the boys how to play, laugh, develop a sense of humor, and they even began to understand sarcasm which was a totally foreign concept. We spent significant time teaching them how to be children and allowing the adults to worry about basic needs such as food and safety.

Family dynamics were taught since they had never seen a functional family unit. We attended family therapy to assist in this area. They learned the role of a mother and father, and how a family functioned together as a unit. This took significant time, but once they discovered the freedom that came with trusting the adults to care for them, they appeared to start enjoying what remained of their childhood. It was a truly amazing gift to sit and watch them play at the park, develop true friendships and begin to experience a typical childhood.

Until adoption was complete academics were not a priority. When a child is stuck in chronic fear, they are only able to focus on primal needs such as food, shelter and maintaining safety. Now that they no longer worried about those necessities, they were able to focus on academics and began to set goals for the first time in their lives. We spent time catching up and filling the academic holes. Over time, they both began to catch up to the level of the other children their age. Both boys were motivated to succeed and had a strong desire to please us.

We continued to spend extensive time in therapy in order to move beyond the significant trauma. Navigating the pain was extremely difficult. As we moved through the pain together, connections were formed and relationships were strengthened. They began to realize that they did not need to journey the path to healing alone; this journey was one we traveled as a family.

Empathy was not a concept they understood. Trent struggled to understand why I would cry when he was hurting deeply from the trauma of his past. Finally, months into our healing journey, he grasped my hand and said, "I finally get it, you are sad because I am sad and that is because you love me". These moments were very powerful and facilitated very teachable moments about relationships, life, and interacting socially with others.

Each of the boys began to heal, but took different paths to do so. As a coping mechanism, Mike remained quiet and very rarely spoke of his past trauma. Since the majority of his abuse occurred before his language developed, he found describing memories to be very difficult. He was often consumed by vague feelings of fear, hunger, and sadness. He learned techniques to handle each of these as they occurred.

Both boys had a strong desire to heal from an early age, but Trent made a definite decision to face every ounce of pain as often as needed in order to move beyond his past. His power and strength were greater than any I ever anticipated. He had a very deep desire to make sense of what happened to him and use it for good in some manner. We knew that moving beyond extreme neglect, domestic violence, and sexual abuse would take a significant amount of time, but he entered the battle with an intense drive to leave his trauma behind. His motivation was unwavering, and he sought deep conversations, began reading on trauma, and frequently engaged in prayer. He developed the vital understanding that nothing that occurred in his past was his fault. He was determined to emerge from his trauma as a strong Christian young man who was going to change the world.

Watch Us Rise

A phoenix is a mythical bird with fiery plumage. When it nears the end of its life, it creates a nest of sticks and twigs that are then set on fire. The bird settles into the burning nest and is quickly reduced to ashes. From those ashes, a beautiful new bird is born. The bird is born healthy, renewed, and ready to face the world.

Our journey was somewhat like the life of a phoenix. We were most certainly hurt by the ferocious fires of anxiety, fear, and doubt and faced raging fires of pain as we faced trauma head on.

Although we were aware that the process may never be complete, a great deal of healing occurred, and we were ready to emerge from the flames that had been all consuming.

God stirred my heart through our entire journey to use our experiences to help others. Thoughts repeatedly entered my mind that we had traveled this painful journey for some sort of purpose. Ready to answer the call, I requested a family meeting and shared the ideas that had been consuming my thoughts. I felt a strong calling to step away from my current job to start a non-profit organization to work on behalf of children in foster care. I had a deep desire to advocate on behalf of the children who were so often overlooked. Without hesitation, Mac agreed that we would take the giant leap of faith and that I would give up my lengthy career to answer God's call.

One month later, I resigned from my seventeen-year career as a special education teacher to start Mercy for America's Children. Our goal was to promote and support adoption of children in foster care with a specific emphasis on the older children.

We embraced this new venture as a family and poured every ounce of money and time into making the organization successful. We prayed that Mercy for America's Children would change lives.

Over the next several years, we watched in amazement as we were able to educate the public about the needs within the foster care system, recruit well over 370 families to adopt through foster care, and develop an extensive list of support services that were available free of charge to families. We had emerged and began to see beauty form from ashes as we followed God's call.

Over time, each family member developed their specific role within the organization. I stepped up to serve as the Founder and Executive Director. Mac serves as the Board Chairman to lead a strong group of individuals. Mike likes to remain out of the spotlight due to his shy personality, but offers his valuable services as our technology assistant and serves diligently behind the scenes. Trent quickly emerged as a true leader and serves on the Board of Directors as a Child Representative. He also spearheaded the development of our Kids Division. Trent began public speaking at the age of ten and spoke openly in over 100 venues by the age of 16. He continues to speak openly about his healing journey in front of crowds of over 2,000. His passion is to share with the world that he is not damaged goods and that true healing can occur through a family that never gives up and leads you to the healing found in God. As a result, he also started a speaking ministry and frequently speaks in churches, civic groups and to adoptive and foster families in order to provide hope.

When shopping one day, Trent picked up an engraved bracelet that had a quote by Rumi. It said, "You have seen my descent, now WATCH ME RISE". This has become his new favorite saying. This hits home on a very emotional level since he once descended deep into the depths of trauma, but he has now risen to heights beyond our wildest dreams.

Trent has been recognized for his efforts by receiving many accolades and awards. Each time he is recognized, he gives God the glory for his healing.

The pain from our journey fades into the distance each time I catch a glimpse of my boys who are now strong, secure, Christian young men who no longer let trauma define them. They are no longer victims of their past; they have learned to view their suffering as part of their journey in life that eventually led them HOME!

REFLECTIONS

As we grasp hands and pray each morning as a family, we often thank God for the painful journey we traveled. Just as the boys have learned to view their pain as part of their journey, I have no question that we experienced each and every painful step for a purpose. I am able to use the knowledge and strength gathered through the process to spend each day helping others navigate the adoption journey. I now have a great sense of fulfillment in doing my job as I am able to walk alongside other families who are experiencing similar suffering. I am able to provide hope and encourage them to hold on and try to enjoy the ride!

Since starting our non-profit organization in 2011, our family has embraced the mission that we feel God has called us to lead. I have sought extensive training in trauma in order to support families in ways that would have helped us. Answering the call to foster or adopt is not an easy one. My goal is to use our story, including both successes and failures, to impact others in a positive way.

The fear of losing the two boys I loved so deeply was the greatest pain I have experienced in my life, but during those darkest moments, I had no choice but to rely solely on God. A great sense of peace came in those moments when I was able to turn every fear over to Him. I learned a total reliance on God that has forever changed me. We can now see that God had a plan from the beginning.

The pain of our personal journey has faded over the years, but the relationships we formed in the midst of the pain are what I treasure. I think the fear of losing them caused me to hold on tighter than what some may view as normal. Our family was formed through non-traditional means and we may always function differently from others. Each of us embrace those differences and love one another very deeply. Journeying through the pain brought us all closer and we value every moment we are able to spend together. Those feelings of potential loss are difficult to release, but they do fade with time.

Smiles and laughter are now a very common occurrence in our home. Now, when I see the smiles, they are no longer masking deep dark pain. They are smiles that demonstrate genuine happiness that is felt when you are loved unconditionally by a family.

Next time I see a bird nest that has been carefully crafted by a mother bird, I will view it a little differently. We have spent the last 8 years carefully crafting a safe nest and have provided them with every ounce of guidance, protection and unconditional love that they will need in order to muster enough confidence to fly. Selfishly, it is my sincere hope that they never fly too far from the nest. However,I know that they are certainly ready to soar! Fly baby birds, fly!